The Windmill Tree

Sally Frances Cazeaux

The Windmill Tree

Copyright © 2012, Sally Frances Cazeaux

All Rights Reserved

ISBN: 978-1-291-04811-7

Contents

Chapter 1 – The Windmill Tree
March 1987- December 1990   7

Chapter 2 – Autism and Miranda
January 1991 – November 1991   25

Chapter 3 – Starting School
November 1991 – June 1992   45

Chapter 4 – To France and Back
July 1992 – December 1992   57

Chapter 5 – Dreadful News about Zöe
January 1993 – April 1993   73

Chapter 6 – To Ronald McDonald House
April 1993 – July 1993   93

Chapter 7 – Disneyland Paris and Afterwards
July 1993 – November 1993   115

Chapter 8 – Hoping for a Miracle
November 1993 – March 1994   135

Chapter 9 – Postcard from Heaven
April 1994 – May 1997   153

Chapter 10 – Just Miranda
April 1994 – December 1999   159

Chapter 11 - A New Millennium
April 2000 – March 2003   169

The Windmill Tree

A Story of Childhood, Life, Death and Autism

Introduction

Our world had changed not once but twice.

Crowds of commuters rushed by on their way to London Bridge Station. Life went on just as it always had done but everything had changed for me. Nothing would ever be the same again.

As I walked towards Guy's Hospital I heard the birds singing.

"How can they sing so beautifully amidst so much sadness?" I wondered.

Miranda sat in her pushchair and screamed. We entered the hospital and walked down the long corridors to see her sister Zöe. I cast my mind back to the time when my two little girls were just babies. The future held so much promise then.

The birds carried on singing and I kept on dreaming that this was all a nightmare and life could be beautiful once again............

Chapter 1 – The Windmill Tree

March 1987 – December 1990

Life is short. Children come into our world shrouded in innocence and we do not know what life has in store for them. We do not know how much joy they will bring or how much sorrow.

Life is short. We must do our best to make the most of every day because it can spiral out of control.

Zöe was born just after 7 a.m on 28th March 1987. She weighed 7lbs 12oz and had a most beautiful complexion and masses of dark wavy hair. She was very lively with heaps of personality from the moment she was born and unlike the other babies in the ward she hardly slept at all.

When Rudi, my husband took us home we were all greeted by a host of golden daffodils in the front garden. Over the next few days a stream of friends and relatives came to see us bringing cards, presents and lots of advice. Life was good and we loved our little daughter very much.

We set up a sleep routine for Zöe but soon found out that she had different ideas. As long as she could sleep on my lap, near her milk supply, she was happy. The moment I lifted her off my lap and put her into the beautiful frilly Moses basket she would wake-up. Everyone had different ideas about how to make babies sleep but very little worked. Sleep remained a major problem. Rudi and I needed lots of it and Zöe did not!

The summer of 1987 was beautiful and sunny. I proudly took Zöe for walks in her pram and showed her off to all the neighbours. In Whitstable as long as you have a baby or a dog people will always stop to say hello to you! When Zöe was three months old she started to say "hello" back to people. At first we could hardly believe this but gradually her "hellos" became clearer and clearer. She loved to be around other people and was very sociable.

It was very exciting to watch our baby grow bigger. We played with her a lot and were delighted when she blew bubbles, sucked her toes or smiled at us. I loved being at home with Zöe and had no desire to return to full-time work. Rudi worked for British Telecom and he commuted by train to London daily. He left for work at 6.30 a.m. and arrived home twelve hours later. It was a long day and in the evenings he often relaxed by playing his keyboard. Zöe loved music and at six months old she would pound away at the keyboard with him, making noises which resembled singing. She had a preference for the black notes but we never found out why.

Generally Zöe seemed healthy but she suffered from ear infections and the occasional bout of sickness. We were told not to worry about this, as there were a lot of viruses about. At Zöe's sixth month check-up, we were told that she had a slight squint. The lady who examined her asked me if she was English. I explained that my parents and I were English but Rudi was French. Zöe also had a Spanish granny and a Bulgarian grandad. The lady then said that maybe Zöe did not have a squint after all but just looked foreign!

At 9 months old, Zöe started to walk without holding on to anything. She looked too tiny to be walking but once she started there was no stopping her. It was December and she loved the Christmas tree, the lights and decorations. We put the tree into her playpen so that she could not pull it over. Zöe was very active and refused to go in a playpen herself.

We loved the outdoors and often walked across the fields to the seaside where we watched the sailing boats and threw pebbles in the sea. Every day Zöe played with other babies and toddlers or we visited her grandparents. She was interested in everything and everyone. Her vocabulary increased very quickly and she pointed at flowers, dogs, cats, cars and people wanting to know what everything was called. When she was at home she would look at picture books and it seemed as if she was absorbing as much information as possible. Our baby was growing up and becoming a beautiful, intelligent little girl. On her first birthday we had a big party with all our friends and then went to a park where the children could run around.

Summer 1988 in Whitstable was wonderful because there was so much going on: Mayday festivities, dancing, regattas, funfairs, parades, oyster festivals and carnivals. The fun never seemed to end. Zöe loved weekends and holidays when Rudi was at home. He would carry her around on his shoulders and play with her for ages.

My sister Olive was married in a beautiful little church across the field from our house. We were all very excited about the wedding especially Zöe. She danced, ran around and posed for the wedding video. She was very impressed by all the beautiful dresses and enjoyed trying everyone's hats on and meeting more relatives.

At about that time, I found out I was pregnant again. We were really pleased as we longed to have a little sister or brother for Zöe to play with. I had strange cravings for red cabbage, mint ice-cream and cherry nougat. Zöe still woke-up every couple of hours during the night and I was exhausted all the time. In the mornings Zöe and I would go out as usual. In the afternoons, we would both curl-up on the sofa and sleep for an hour or so. Zöe was kind, thoughtful and eager to help me. She seemed to understand that I was extra tired as I was having a baby. Once she unpacked my shopping into the kitchen cupboards and when she ran out of space, she put the rest of it into the washing machine. She would pick daisies for me when we walked through the fields to the shops and she would sing me songs. Zöe was my little friend as well as my daughter! I wondered how a new little sister would affect our close relationship.

In November 1988, we went to Spain on holiday. This was a big adventure and we were all excited. The flight seemed long with an active toddler but at the hotel Zöe slept soundly, without waking-up. This was the first time ever that she had slept through the night. The next day she was very, very sick. We had to buy her new clothes because we ran out of clean ones to dress her in. By night-time she seemed to have recovered and danced for ages with me at the hotel disco. All the guests made a fuss of her because she had been so ill. Zöe looked very pretty with her long dark wavy hair and big brown eyes. She loved all the attention.

The following day, I became very sick and could not leave the hotel room. Then the sickness spread to Rudi. We found out that lots of people at the hotel were suffering from the so-called "Spanish tummy." There was a cooking oil scare and many people were being very ill. After a couple of days, we all felt better and made the most of our holiday. We visited zoos, swing parks, the mountains and the seaside. Zöe played happily with all the Spanish children we met and I could not help but notice how Spanish she looked.

When we arrived back in England, I went straight to the doctor and had a scan. I was worried that the sickness had affected the new baby growing inside me. Everything seemed to be okay.

In January 1989 Zöe was very ill. We worried as she had lost a lot of weight. The doctor came and said it was probably another virus and gave her antibiotics. After a few days she was running around and active again. However, Zöe's personality seemed to have changed. She had tantrums every day at the smallest of things. She refused to let me dress her. I would put her shoes on and she would take them off again. She would insist on wearing one blue shoe and one red shoe when we went out. She would fight like crazy with other toddlers to get the toys she wanted and once she had them she did not want them anymore.

Every little thing we tried to get her to do was difficult. She would throw herself on the floor and bang her head whenever she could not get her way. None of the other parents or the health visitors seemed worried by this. I was told that this was all normal toddler behaviour. Sure enough, this phase only lasted a few months and then I had my friendly little girl back again.

Meanwhile the new baby was growing bigger. Zöe was delighted that I was pregnant. She would press my tummy and say "up and down baby" and put water into my belly button to give the baby a wash. When it kicked she told me that the baby was playing football inside me. She wanted it to be bigger so it could come out.

In February, I had another scan and some blood tests at the hospital. We were told that the new baby would probably be smaller than Zöe had been. I was told to rest as much as possible so the baby could get more oxygen and as it kept changing position I had to go for regular check-ups at the hospital. I was very worried in case something was wrong. I was also anxious about leaving Zöe if I had to go into hospital for a long time. I adored her and my time with her was precious.

On Wednesday 12th April, for the first time in ages, I had an amazing surge of energy. I recognised this as a sign that the baby would be arriving soon. Zöe told me that if my waters broke she would ask daddy to mend them. During the evening I felt a trickle of water run down my leg and I knew the baby was coming. Zöe brought some toys, a balloon and a blanket. She gave me her favourite green and yellow spotted ball to take to hospital as a present for the baby when it came out. After all it had been kicking inside my tummy for months so she figured out that the baby would be a footballer. We did not know if it was a boy or a girl.

Rudi, Zöe and I left for the hospital about 10.30 p.m. We waited for ages at the level crossing in Canterbury for a train to pass. Zöe was very excited about this but I was worried that I would have the baby in the car. At the hospital I was taken to the labour room. Rudi and Zöe both paced the corridors until we all realised I had left my suitcase at home. They went home to fetch it and returned later on. By that time, Zöe was tired and so Rudi left me at the hospital and took her home to sleep. I had a relaxing bath and felt quite calm about the baby coming. As the contractions became stronger I decided to get out of the water. I was dubious about having a baby in the bath especially as I had put in lots of bubble bath! I had an easy birth and Miranda came into the world calmly at 2.35 a.m. on April 13th 1989. I fed her and gave her a cuddle. I never had much sleep that night but Miranda seemed very content to sleep or just look around. I phoned everyone to tell them the news. We were all delighted. Our life seemed almost perfect.

Miranda had a tiny cry. She was a lot less nervous than Zöe when she was born and did not jump quite as much when the hospital trolleys clattered passed or when the staff banged about and vacuumed. She seemed very small at only 6lbs 4ozs and was very fair with blue-green eyes.

Zöe and Rudi came to see me the next morning. Zöe pointed at my tummy and said "baby not in there." Then she pointed to the cot and said "baby in there." She seemed excited to have a sister but a little bewildered and clung to Rudi and her toy rabbit.

The next day we brought Miranda home and my parents came to see her. Zöe kept touching her and saying "Miranda, my sister." My parents played with Zöe and helped with the housework whilst Rudi cooked the meals and I looked after Miranda. I was careful to give Zöe lots of attention too as I suspected she was feeling jealous. Zöe decided she wanted to have her afternoon sleep next to Rudi and not with me. She did not like it when I breast-fed Miranda and looked so hurt that I felt guilty. She wanted a cuddle whenever I fed Miranda and occasionally would give me a smack and tell me to take Miranda away.

Fortunately when Zöe's best friend came to visit she was much more interested in playing with Zöe than seeing a new baby which helped the jealousy situation. A few weeks after Miranda was born Zöe sat up in bed and said "I like my sister." This was a turning point and suddenly she seemed to accept Miranda instead of seeing her as an attention-seeking nuisance! From then onwards she would bring her toys, give her cuddles and gently stroke her. We had our first outing to a toddler group and Zöe seemed quite proud of Miranda when she watched the other mothers making a fuss of her. Miranda stayed very quiet and seemed completely happy to be passed around and for everyone to come and have a look at her.

Both children loved the outdoors and the summer of 1989 was glorious. We spent a lot of time in my parent's garden. Miranda would lie happily in her pram listening to the leaves rustling on their large tree. Zöe loved to play with buckets of water and to do the gardening. She helped her granny plant lots of sprouting potatoes and every few days she would dig them up to see if any new baby potatoes were growing.

We acquired a slide, a tent and a large paddling pool for our back garden and lots of Zöe's friends came to play. We went on outings to farms, swing parks and the seaside. We visited Margate and Zöe was fascinated by the feel of soft fine sand beneath her feet. She thought it was wonderful compared to Whitstable's pebbly beaches. She had her first pink, white and green ice-cream, paddled in the sea, made sandcastles and went on lots of musical cars and children's seaside rides. Miranda was content to just lie in her pram and enjoy the summer sunshine.

Our toddler group had an outing to Minnis Bay. All the children ran around with bright shiny windmills and this inspired Zöe and I to make a windmill tree. We had a tree with only one leaf and no blossom at the back of our garden, which we could see from the patio doors. We tied lots of windmills onto the branches so that when the wind blew they would whirl around. It became a very popular tree.

Zöe passed her two year check with flying colours and she impressed the health visitor by doing many things that three and four year olds do. She was bright, vivacious, sociable and eager to learn.

Miranda had her polio, whooping cough, tetanus and dipheria injection. She was usually a very healthy, happy baby however she was upset by the injection and cried for a long time. She seemed unwell afterwards. Zöe was very sympathetic. She called her "Mimanda Jayne" or "pudding" and told everyone that her sister was "gorgeous".

When Zöe was two and a half we took her to Nursery School to see if she would like it. Her older friends already went there. Zöe sobbed bitterly when we left her and told everyone she missed us, so we decided to keep her at home for another year. After all, there was no hurry for her to grow-up.

Autumn 1989 came and Miranda started to become mobile. She managed to crawl forwards, after going backwards and round and round for a long time! She also did push-ups and swimming movements on the floor but best of all we loved to see her bunny hops. Miranda would bounce on the spot for a few moments before taking off and going round in circles. Doing this would keep Miranda amused for ages. She was happy to stay in the same area and not very eager to explore at all. I thought what an easy baby she was compared to Zöe who had always been very energetic and adventurous.

Rudi and I were continually tired as both girls woke-up frequently in the night but when they did sleep the girls looked so peaceful and beautiful that all the exhaustion seemed worthwhile.

Rudi and I regularly took the children to a Mormon Church. We had both joined the religion before we met. On our bedroom wall we had a big picture of the Temple where we were married. This was a place where church members had ceremonies, which they believed were not just for on this earth but for all eternity – this life and the next. One evening Miranda, Zöe and I were sitting in the bedroom. Zöe looked at the picture of the temple and asked, "Who is the lady in the picture?"

There was no lady in the picture – it was purely a picture of the temple building and the grounds around it.
I said to Zöe, "Can you see a lady?"
She said, "Yes".

"What does she look like?"
"Big."
"Is she nice?"
"Yes."
"What's her name?"
"I don't know."
It was spooky. Zöe really seemed to see a lady in the picture but there was no-one there. I turned all the lights on and went downstairs.

A few times after that Zöe would tell me things before they happened.
"Grandad's car is coming," she would say.
I would like out of the window and see no cars at all. Then his car would come around the corner. It was strange.

We had cold winter weather. Zöe kept being sick and we were told she had picked-up yet another virus. It did not seem right but the doctor was not worried. However, the sickness carried on. Zöe was being sick every couple of weeks, so I took her to the doctor again. She had turned yellow which was very worrying. When she was first born she had jaundice for a few days and I wondered if she had it again.

"I'm afraid your child has a drink problem," the doctor told me with a twinkle in his eye, "the beta-carotene in all the orange juice she has been drinking is turning her yellow."

Zöe did drink a lot of orange squash and juices. It was so unusual to see a yellow child that the student doctors at the surgery came in to have a look at her. We had to stop the orange drinks and give her water instead. Sure enough she went back to her normal colour.

I took Zöe for another eye test and was told that her eyesight was good. Apparently she had an eye which looked "lazy" but she could see well out of it. However, a few days later Zöe had an accident and I wondered how accurate the eye test had been. She had leapt from her a chair and hit her head on the wall. There

15

was blood everywhere and I panicked. Rudi was at work and I was alone with the two children.

I phoned my sister Olive and she came round to mind Miranda. Fortunately our friend Pauline turned up just after the accident and she took us in her car to the hospital. We wrapped a towel around Zöe's head and she went to sleep. When we arrived at the casualty department she woke-up full of energy and raced around talking quite happily. We were lucky she did not need stitches. It was Zöe's second trip to Casualty. A few months before she had been racing around the church and hurt her toe badly. She was very active but also a little accident-prone we thought.

At seven months old Miranda would follow me around everywhere. She started to say a few baby words, "dada, mama and hello," but her speech was not as clear or as frequent as Zöe's had been. We decided that now Miranda was getting bigger, she should have a room of her own. Zöe already had her own bedroom. In theory this was a good idea but in practice both children woke up a lot and I spent most nights walking from one room to another.

Miranda suffered from tonsillitis and then she had problems with ear infections and sticky eyes. In December, when Miranda was eight months old, we took her for a routine hearing test. She deliberately refused to co-operate and looked away from the sounds all the time. The table in the middle of the room seemed to fascinate Miranda. She would often deliberately ignore people and focus on objects. The health visitor said they would try to test her again in a few months' time.

Christmas was coming and Zöe was very excited. I gave her a clue to one of her Christmas presents. It was a spinning top so I told her it went round and round.

"Oh, it's a round-a-bout for the back garden," she said.

The children were ill again when Christmas day arrived and Zöe had lots of tantrums. She would scream, shout and stamp her feet if she did not feel well or when she could not have her own way. We were all tired and worried about Zöe's health. She still did not sleep properly, sometimes waking up nine times in one night. She seemed small, thin and frail.

At the baby clinic the Health Visitor weighed both the children. Zöe was underweight and small for a child who was nearly three years old. Miranda was doing well for nine months old or so it seemed. However, she was ill again following her third set of baby injections. She seemed to react badly to childhood vaccinations.

I started to take driving lessons. If I could learn to drive it would be easier to get around with two small children especially as we lived a long way from the Health Centre and shops.

Miranda started to walk at eleven months old. Unlike Zöe she was very cautious and made slow progress, just a few steps at a time. An occupational therapist came to visit us and discussed the children's sleep problems. She told us to put Miranda to bed in her cot wide-awake and let her cry until she went to sleep. We were not to go in and comfort her. Against our instincts we followed her advice and listened to Miranda crying for ages. After an hour, I went into her bedroom and found Miranda fast asleep with one leg and one arm hanging over the top of the cot bars. She had fallen asleep whilst trying to climb out.

No-one had any idea what to do about Zöe who still was waking up a lot and having the occasional night-time terrors. Sometimes she would stare into space and throw things at us such as teddy-bears and pillows. I realised she was often still half-asleep and having nightmares. Occasionally she seemed to twitch slightly in her sleep.

Things became worse and Miranda started to wake up at two o'clock in the morning and would remain awake until the following evening. This happened about three times a week. I had to take her downstairs so she did not disturb Rudi or Zöe and our neighbours who were very understanding. Sometimes

Miranda would scream in the middle of the night. I tried various things to get her back to sleep. People had lots of suggestions such as playing dolphin noises to calm her or recording her screams and playing them back to her. None of the suggestions worked. The doctor prescribed sleeping medicine for both girls. It made them sleep but they woke-up very grumpy the next day.

When Zöe was three years old we had a lovely birthday party and all her friends came. We put the children's slide and play-tent in the garden and they all played outside. Miranda's first birthday was two weeks later in April. She was quite content to play with the few toys that she liked and to watch everyone around her. Her favourite toys were ones which you could hit things with – rubber hammers, plastic skittles and drumsticks. She loved to have a cuddle from us and babbled quite happily but only said one word now, "Dadda."

We often used to take the children to a nearby caravan site where there was a children's playground. Zöe loved to go on everything and would always make friends with the children who were on holiday there but Miranda viewed everything and everyone with caution. She was only one year old so it did not worry us that she seemed slightly unsociable. Zöe loved to visit people and would be restless if she stayed indoors more than one day. Miranda would amuse herself with one toy or one book for ages and loved being at home. It was amazing that they were so completely different.

Our best days out were on the shingle beach near our house. The girls would play for hours with the shiny pebbles and splash about in puddles of mud. Occasionally we would find a patch of sand and build a sandcastle. Zöe would laugh at the number of pebbles that ended up inside Miranda's baggy nappy. We would shake them out and I would push the girls home in a double buggy. Those blissful days by the sea made up for all the times when we had illness, tantrums and sleepless nights.

We took the girls on a day trip to France in May. Rudi took the day off and my mother came to help. Miranda ran round and round the boat then put her arms around Zöe and gave her a big hug. This was a new thing and we were delighted to see her show her love for her sister. On the boat there was a special room with a ball pit where the children could play. They had a wonderful time in there. A photographer took Zöe's picture and asked if she could put it on the cover of a new holiday brochure coming out soon. Zöe looked beautiful and was very excited at the thought of being famous.

We found a furniture shop in Canterbury with a large rocket filled with similar coloured balls for children to play in. I would wheel Miranda round and round looking at settees whilst Zöe frolicked about in the rocket of balls. Miranda would not go into the rocket. We never did buy any furniture from the shop but the staff did not seem to mind our regular visits.

We became involved with some people who were helping Romanian orphanages and started to collect baby clothes and toys to send out to the children. We had a sale in our back garden to raise money for the orphans.

"They can have my toys," said Zöe generously, "but not my mummy and daddy."

Miranda was becoming a very clingy toddler. She would hang onto my leg when I walked around the house and continually want to be picked-up. I felt like a mummy bear with a little cub constantly attached to me. I was told it was normal for a one year old to be possessive. I was still breastfeeding Miranda and felt quite embarrassed about it because she was so big. I tried to cut out her feeds one at a time but she would cry for ages whenever a feed was due. Eventually I just stopped breastfeeding her completely and we all put up with a few days of tears and tantrums. It was great for me to have more freedom and have my body back at last!

At sixteen months old Miranda had her measles, mumps and rubella injection. As usual she screamed and reacted badly to it. We took her for another hearing test shortly afterwards. It showed that Miranda could hear but she chose to ignore sounds when she wanted to. She still was not speaking except for a very occasional unclear word. Some of our friends wondered if she was deaf. Miranda often ignored people and sometimes would go upstairs and hide when children came to play. Her behaviour was becoming odder. We were told that a more detailed examination would be arranged.

In September 1990, I took Zöe to Nursery School again. We walked across the fields to the church hall in Faversham Road where it was held. This time I felt sure she would like it as most of her friends went there. I felt sad when I left Zöe and walked away. She had put on her favourite dress and I could feel her excitement and nervousness. I walked on with Miranda in the pushchair to our regular toddler group and then afterwards took her to the swing park nearby. Miranda never wanted to go on anything there. She just stood still for ages in a little wooden playhouse. I missed having Zöe walking beside me, chatting away and holding my hand.

Before she went to Nursery School she said to me, "Now you can have your peace and quiet."

I felt really guilty because of all the times when I'd said "I'll be pleased to have some peace and quiet when you go to Nursery School."

There are many things that mothers say when they are tired but do not really mean.

When I collected Zöe she was very happy and had enjoyed her morning. She told me she listened to the story of "The Three Little Pigs". She had played with farm animals and been on a slide, a trampoline and a climbing frame. Rudi phoned to see how Zöe was and she told him all about it. We were very proud of her.

Zöe discovered rainbows and was fascinated by them. Her grandmother held up a crystal glass in front of the windows and made rainbows indoors for Zöe. Her granny always had new games to play with Zöe and exciting stories to tell her. Zöe loved to dress-up in her granny's jewellery, put lipstick on and drape chiffon scarves around her waist.

Zöe and her granny were the best of friends and would often go to feed the horses in the field near our house. On one particular occasion her granny took Zöe across the field to the little stone church and cemetery. A little boy was standing and talking to himself and Zöe asked him what he was doing.

"I'm talking to my granny," he said. "She died and she's buried under the ground."

Zöe thought about this for a moment and said, "Granny when you die, I'm going to come and talk to you."

I took Miranda to the Health Centre for another hearing test – a more complex one. Miranda knew something was up the moment we arrived there. The lady who tested her was a hearing specialist and also a teacher of deaf children. Miranda sat on my lap and the examiner made noises behind us. She responded to 45 decibels and above which I was told was average. She tested Miranda for different pitches and I was told she could hear quite a normal range of sounds although she had excessive fluid in the ears. Miranda did not want to co-operate and had a screaming tantrum. I gave her a packet of quavers to calm her down so the lady could finish the test but I was told off for doing that. I had broken the golden rule: you must not reward children who have tantrums even if it is to get a hearing test finished. The conclusion of the hearing test was that Miranda had some fluid in her ears but her hearing seemed normal. The lady testing her suggested that her development was slow and something else could be wrong. She was not sure what and I felt worried.

The next day I had a dreadful migraine and was sick. The children sensed I was ill and played quite happily without wanting a lot of attention. Zöe took her playhouse apart and then played with a large cardboard box. Miranda spent the day shredding up toilet paper and kitchen rolls. I felt so ill I did not care about the mess and destruction around me.

October came and I had my fiftieth driving lesson. It was to be my last. After I nearly hit a car the driving instructor advised me to stop learning to drive! This was my third driving teacher. I had hated every lesson and agreed that I was not cut-out to be a driver. I was disappointed as it would have been easier to get out and about with the children in a car rather than struggling everywhere with a pushchair and I felt guilty about all the money spent on lessons.

When I arrived home after the driving lesson, I decided to take the children to the sea. It was only a few minutes' walk away and a lovely sunny day. We crossed a humped bridge and walked down a steep and narrow slope to the beach. It was hard pushing a double buggy. Miranda played in a pool of mud as the tide was out, soaking her shoes, socks and trousers as she splashed around. The people who walked passed laughed as she was having so much fun. Zöe and I looked for crabs and collected shells.

I noticed a man standing next to the footpath we had walked down to the beach. He was acting strangely, touching his trousers and watching the people on the beach. Instinctively I felt we were in danger. The other people nearby must have felt the same because the beach cleared in seconds and just the children and I were left there. I dragged Miranda out of the muddy pools, not bothering to dry her or change her clothes. I said to Zöe that we had to go straightaway. For once neither of the children complained about leaving so soon. They could sense the urgency in my voice.

We walked up to the double buggy at the top of the beach and the children sat down. The strange man was standing next to it and blocked my path as I tried to move the pushchair. Then he insisted on helping us to the top of the slope. I could tell he was disturbed in some way and tried to talk him into leaving us alone but to no avail. He pushed the buggy very hard and the children bumped about. There were tall hedges on both sides of the slope so that no-one could see us. I began to panic and I hoped that someone else would come along but no-one did. The man was sweating heavily and kept touching me. When we reached the top of the slope he grabbed me and tried to kiss me. I somehow managed to get away and pushed the children home quickly. We called the police but they never found the man. Zöe was puzzled and upset by what had happened and knew it was wrong of a strange man to grab hold of me. I hoped she would forget the incident. Rudi was very concerned and I realised that I spent a lot of time walking about with the children in fairly isolated places, across fields and on the beach. I would have to be careful. It was ironic that this had happened on the day of my last ever driving lesson. I felt limited as to where I could take the girls when I was at home without Rudi to drive the car.

Winter was coming and with it the cold weather. Zöe was always hot and kept taking her warm clothes off. I felt embarrassed when people commented on it. She liked to wear summer dresses whatever the weather. We wondered if it was normal for a child to feel so hot all the time. However, I remembered taking my hat and coat off on the way to school as soon as I was out of my mother's sight and concluded that children do not always feel the cold in the same way as adults do.

In December Zöe came home from Nursery School with a Christmas calendar, a hyacinth in a pot and a moving Father Christmas. She told me that she had dressed up in a white thing and had a decoration put on her head. I suspected she was going to be a Christmas angel in the nativity play. Her best friend was an angel too and the little boy who lived next door was a king. The play was wonderful and the children loved acting. Zöe sat proudly behind Mary and Baby Jesus. She kept bobbing up and down and smiling at us. Later, she told us the Christmas story.

We went to see Father Christmas at the Nursery School. Miranda was frightened when he asked the children to shout out the answers to questions. She did not like the noise and banged her head with frustration. She was doing this a lot and we worried that she would hurt herself. Her tantrums were far worse than Zöe's ones had been and they were much more frequent.

I took Zöe to see Father Christmas at Ricemans store in Canterbury. When he asked her what she wanted for Christmas she said, "sausages."

"That was a funny thing to say." I remarked as we left the shop. "Well, how I was meant to know what to say?" Zöe replied.

We went to a Christmas Bazaar at the Women's Institute Hall and Zöe chose a pair of red earrings for her granny. It was her own idea and I felt proud of her for being so thoughtful at such a young age.

That year the girls were ill on Christmas Day again. I wondered if any families really had the type of joyous Christmas that we watch on the old films with everyone laughing and happy. At least we could enjoy having Rudi at home during the Christmas holidays. It was wonderful when he did not have to commute to London and we could all spend time together. When he went back to work we all missed him being around. I hoped that the girls would be healthier and less worrying in 1991.

Chapter 2 – Autism and Miranda

January 1991- November 1991

Miranda kicked me and screamed. I was talking to our doctor and she made it quite clear that she did not want to be there. He smiled and told me that I should buy some cricket pads to wear on my legs because of her kicking. It was January 1991 and Miranda was 21 months old.

Both of Miranda's ears were infected so he gave her antibiotics. He asked me a lot of questions about Miranda and told me that he was referring her to The Mary Sheridan Centre in Canterbury for an assessment as she was not speaking yet and might need speech therapy. I had told him how unsociable she was and how different from Zöe at that age. Then he looked at me very seriously and suggested that maybe Miranda was not developing normally. I turned cold and panicked inside when he said this - I suspected something was wrong as well and I was really worried.

Miranda's appointment at The Mary Sheridan Centre was on 4th February, two months before her second birthday. I was told to sit with her in the waiting room and wait for the doctor. Miranda was quite excited. She played with a few toys, studied the fish tank for a while and then started to spin herself around like a spinning top. Miranda loved to spin and it surprised me that she did not seem to get dizzy. This seemed an odd behaviour but I was pleased she could amuse herself so well. When the doctor came into the room she told me to stop Miranda spinning at once.

We followed the doctor into a large room which looked more like a nursery than a surgery. This was good as Miranda was not frightened at first and seemed quite relaxed. I had to answer loads of questions about our backgrounds and our social activities. This puzzled me as we had an excellent social life and the questions seemed strange.

Then Miranda had to do a series of tests such as brushing a dolls hair, putting shapes into a shape sorter and drawing. I presumed the doctor was testing her to see if she could understand and obey instructions. Miranda was very disobedient and would only do what she wanted to.

The doctor said that she wanted to test Miranda's communication skills. She tried to make Miranda listen to her and look her straight in the eye. This was a very big problem. Miranda was determined not to communicate. She shut her eyes and turned her head to avoid making any eye contact with the doctor. She also put her hands over her ears to block out any words that the doctor said or any noises that she made.

I said that Miranda did not point, wave or make gestures. Simple instructions such as "come here" were beyond her understanding. If she wanted me to get her something she would usually scream and I would try to guess what she was telling me.

"I think she's autistic," the doctor said. She did not explain what "autistic" meant and when I asked her, she said that she did not like to label children or diagnose them at an early age. She told me that Miranda was very young and it was hard to judge how much she would progress. She seemed to regret using the word "autistic" and I felt very uneasy. I did not understand what it meant or what the implications were.

She asked me to tell her more about Miranda. I explained that I did not know which of her behaviours were abnormal and which ones were just because she was a toddler. The doctor said to tell her some of the things I had noticed that slightly worried me about Miranda.

I said she was very possessive towards me, often running to me for security and cuddling up to me. She liked it when I was at home with her alone and she could have me all to herself. Miranda was not very happy when we had lots of visitors.

The doctor said that Miranda would probably be afraid in lots of situations in life and come to me for security. She would probably dislike changes to her normal routine and it was quite likely that she would be frightened of certain people and social situations. She said we might have problems taking her on holiday because that would be a major change and a lot for Miranda to cope with.

I told her that Miranda very rarely played with her sister Zöe or other children. She liked to play on her own when she was not clinging to me or to watch what the others were doing but not join in with them. Miranda loved being by herself and never seemed to be bored. She often laughed for ages for no apparent reason and seemed quite happy amusing herself. I told her how Miranda especially seemed to like repetitive activities and would spend ages climbing in and out of her pushchair and laughing. As a baby she had bunny-hopped round and round in circles.

I mentioned that Miranda did not seem to understand other people's feelings. For example if another child was crying Miranda would be puzzled and might be angry with them.

Miranda would not always tell us if she was in pain herself. If she fell over and cut her knee for example she would just carry on playing despite it bleeding.

She also would hit her head with her hands in frustration or bang her head on the floor when she was upset. She did not become upset for the same reasons as other children. For instance, Miranda was upset when doors were shut or opened. She liked the doors inside our house to be left open at certain angles. She was upset by things like washing powder adverts on television but we could not understand why. She did not like the feel of sand under her feet on the beach but was fine walking on pebbles or stones.

What worried me greatly was that Miranda had given up a lot of the foods that she had eaten as a baby. I tried her with lots of different flavours and textures but she refused to eat a varied diet.

In fact she only ate about five different foods now. Most people said this was a normal phase that toddlers went through, but I thought it seemed extreme

I had also noticed that Miranda liked things to be in order and tidy. She often lined up her toys especially her Thomas the Tank Engine train collection. She liked to build towers with all the cans in my kitchen cupboard. She preferred using real cans to toy bricks. When she had finished with them she would put all the cans back into exactly the same places as before and shut the kitchen cupboard doors. When we were in the garden Miranda tried to tidy up the fallen petals and put them back on the old flowers. She tried to open up the flowers that were still in bud.

I mentioned as well that Miranda would not look at a book in a normal way. She would just study one page in particular in each book and it would always be the same page. Whatever book I gave her she just turned to her chosen page and stared at it for ages.

After we had discussed Miranda, the doctor asked her to walk up and down the stairs. She walked up them but then got hysterical and would not walk down. It was traumatic for her and I carried her back to the assessment room. Miranda was too upset to co-operate after that and the doctor stopped testing her for a while until she calmed down.

Then it was time for Miranda to have another hearing test. This time her hearing seemed normal but the doctor could not be absolutely certain. Miranda seemed to be acting as if she was deaf but she could hear some very quiet noises. She seemed to dislike certain pitches of sound.

I was told that Miranda would definitely need speech therapy to try and help her communicate. The doctor also told me that singing nursery rhymes to Miranda might also help her speech to develop. Often children picked up words from songs.

The doctor gave me plenty of advice as to how I could help Miranda's development. I was to stop her spinning herself round as it was a form of self-stimulation that was not good for her. When Miranda was by herself or focused on an activity, such as looking at a book I was to interrupt her every few minutes and make her play a pretend game with me. As she did not play in a normal way, I needed to stimulate her imagination and teach her how to play. I was to sit in front of her and make her look me in the eyes – it was important to get Miranda to make eye contact with me.

The doctor gave me some ideas of games to try and make Miranda play: putting dolls to bed and covering them with blankets, giving dolls a bath, combing their hair, giving toys a ride in a toy car and having pretend tea parties etc. Miranda usually did not play with dolls. She liked to hold lots of little Duplo people between her fingers but she just carried them around and did nothing else with them.

I was also told to get Miranda to interact more with other people as well as me but this was easier said than done. When I got home, I made a list of possible games we could play with her: blowing bubbles, playing music on a keyboard, playing ball, putting rings on a stick, shapes in a shape sorter, skittles, building cups, putting Duplo people in a truck, chasing games, ring-a-roses, hide and seek, cookery.

I had lots of ideas and hoped that Zöe and the other children would join in and teach Miranda to play more normally. I had to remember to ask everyone who talked to Miranda to face her and look her straight in the eyes when they were speaking. I felt bad that I had never realized eye contact was important or that Miranda did not make eye contact.

Rudi was heart-broken to learn that Miranda might be autistic. He spent ages on the phone to his family in France to find out if there was any history of autism in his family. There was not. No-one in my family knew much about autism either in fact hardly any of us had even heard of the word before. Rudi and I told a few close friends that Miranda could be autistic. It was hard to understand and explain to people what the word meant exactly.

One friend said "Are you sure the doctor said Autistic and not Artistic."

A couple of friends believed the doctor's diagnosis was wrong because Miranda was so pretty and looked normal. We could not get the word "autistic" out of our minds. I decided that maybe it would be better to just tell people that Miranda might have a mild hearing problem and then see how she progressed. I needed to know more about autism before I could tell everyone what it was anyway. I especially did not want Miranda to be labelled as "autistic" when she was not even two years old.

That winter it snowed and the world seemed beautiful outside. The children loved the snow. While they happily watched the snowflakes falling I phoned the Kent Autistic Trust, The National Autistic Society in London and the doctor I had seen at the assessment centre. I needed to know more about autism and what it meant. There was no-one available to phone back so I wrote a letter to the National Autistic Society asking for information. I wanted to know if Miranda was brain damaged. Would a blood test show up autism? What caused autism? Was it curable? Would it affect any other children we had? What was the chromosome test the doctor had mentioned that Miranda might need to have? Would Miranda be able to go to a normal school? I wished I had asked the doctor more questions at the assessment but I had not really taken in everything until afterwards.

Rudi took some time off work and we took turns to play with Miranda and make eye contact with her. The snow was bad and it was difficult to travel to London so Rudi was especially pleased to be at home. We tried to ensure that Zöe would not feel left out while we played with Miranda. Rudi made an enormous snowman for the girls and we fed the birds in the garden. There was a robin who came into our garden regularly and that week the seagulls were also swooping down for food. Miranda loved the birds. One seagull kept flying into our patio window. He did seem to have the strength to make it over our garden fence to the field outside. I picked him up carefully amidst his protests and helped him to fly over the fence to freedom. He was the seagull who needed the extra bit of help to progress on life's journey – maybe a bit like Miranda.

A week passed by. A lady from The Kent Autistic Trust phoned me and answered lots of my questions about autism. She especially reassured me that nothing I had done would have caused the autism. It could not be caused by watching too much television and I had not caused it by stopping Miranda's breastfeeding suddenly after fourteen months. The lady told me that autism affected children in many different ways. Some children were severely affected and needed lots of help and others were very mildly affected. There was no way you could predict how much progress a child would make. The National Autistic Society sent me some books, which I read from cover to cover. I hoped that it was all a big mistake and she was just a slow developer! I made a list of behaviours that applied to Miranda and could indicate autism. The list was as follows:

Bad communication skills
Poor eye contact
Unsociability
Obsessive and repetitive behaviour
Difficulty in mixing with other children
Acting as if deaf
Resistance to learning anything new
No fear of real dangers
Not liking changes or routines
Inappropriate laughing and giggling
Extreme physical over-activity or extreme under-activity
Inappropriate attachment to objects e.g. holding little objects all day
Spinning herself around
Not understanding how other people feel e.g. why they are crying
Not waving, pointing or using gestures
Strange fears of everyday objects or situations

Lining toys or objects up or playing with toys the same way every time
Intense concentration when playing or doing an activity
Hurting self with frustration
Being more interested in objects than people

I took Miranda to a Tupperware party and she spent ages putting all the biscuits down my friend's toilet whilst I was talking and not watching her. One of the older children eventually came to tell us. Miranda did not seem to realise this was naughty but just seemed happy watching the biscuits float and dissolve. The other children and toddlers seemed amused by Miranda. She did not fit in but it was hard to pinpoint exactly why.

I minded a friend's nine year old daughter and she told me that there was an autistic unit at her school. I asked about the children there and she said they seemed naughty. I phoned the school and they were surprised that I had not had the word "autism" fully explained to me when Miranda was assessed. I phoned my local doctor in hope that he would discuss Miranda with me but he told me to wait until he received a letter from the assessment centre about her, then he would contact me. Eventually a phone call came from the doctor's secretary at the assessment centre. She asked Rudi and me to come and talk to her the next day so she could explain the autism diagnosis and what it meant in Miranda's case.

We went back to The Mary Sheridan Centre and spent an hour and a half discussing Miranda. The doctor told us that a lot of Miranda's developmental skills were normal for a two year old. Her speech and communication skills, however, were not even as good as those of a one year old child. She hoped that Miranda would be able to go to a normal school but have extra help from a speech and language unit. However she could not be sure as no-one could predict Miranda's progress or development.

Rudi and I gradually told everyone about Miranda and autism. It was becoming more and more obvious that deafness was not her problem but I still secretly hoped the diagnosis of autism was wrong. The reaction continued to be a mixed one with most people not believing that anything could be wrong with Miranda. People all knew friends with an autistic trait whether it was a certain obsession or a degree of unsociability. It seemed that what made a person "autistic" were the number of autistic traits they had and the intensity of them. Anxiety, obsessions, poor communication and unsociability seemed to be severe problems for many autistic people all of their lives.

Meanwhile, Zöe's friends continued to come and play. At one time they all crawled around the floor opening and shutting their mouths.

"What are you doing?" I asked.

"We are playing autistic dogs." Zöe said. "We are like Miranda. She can't talk and we can't bark."

Zöe's left eye had continued to turn inwards and was affecting her vision. Our doctor referred us to the local eye hospital. The consultant told us that both her eyes had muscles that worked too fast and were too strong. He said Zöe's eyes were working separately and not together so she was not focusing correctly.

In about three months she would need to have one or both eyes operated on. Meanwhile she had to wear a patch over one eye. Zöe broke down in tears the first time we put the eye patch on. Rudi, Miranda and I were all really upset as well. She had to wear it for three hours at first and for certain amounts of time every day thereafter. We tried all sorts of things to make her feel better including buying her pirates eye patches to put on top and drawing faces on the patch. After a few days she got used to wearing a patch and no longer complained.

Zöe was four in March and asked me to make her a large birthday cake in the shape of a tree. She had lots of friends round and we played party games.

Miranda was two years old in April and I made her a birthday cake with a picture of a yellow duck in a pink bonnet iced on the top. Miranda was very excited about it. She loved ducks and birds.

Her birthday party did not start off very well. She screamed for twenty minutes when everyone arrived and then went to sleep but later she woke-up and ran around with the other children quite cheerfully.

We had lots of balloons, played pass-the-parcel and other musical games then the children played on the slide and in our large push-a-long car. Two children would go inside the car, two would sit on the roof, one on bonnet and two on the boot. It was strong and did not tip over! Miranda's favourite presents were little Duplo men. She carried the little people everywhere she went and it was difficult to get her to put them down, even to eat.

When everyone sang "Happy Birthday" to Miranda, she seemed to understand it was a special day. She smiled and was very happy. Our friends all knew that we were trying to get Miranda to play imaginatively. She received eight toy teapots for her birthday and numerous cups and saucers! Rudi and I laughed about it as we never drank tea or used a teapot but we were pleased everyone wanted to help Miranda play imaginative games and have pretend tea-parties.

I started to take Miranda to more toddler groups while Zöe was at Nursery school so that she could meet more children and hopefully become more sociable. Most of the churches in Whitstable held toddler groups on one or more mornings in the week. However, I always found the same thing that Miranda would play with the toys at the groups but not with the other children!

In May there was another assessment to see how Miranda was progressing. She did not spin herself around anymore which was good. However, if she was feeling very excited she would jump up and down repeatedly with her two feet together so it seemed as if one repetitive action had replaced another.

Miranda had learned to go upstairs on her own but she would only walk down if I was holding her hand. She liked to play peep-bo, chasing games or hide and seek with Zöe. She enjoyed having piggy backs with Rudi. Sometimes she would roll a ball back to us if we threw it to her, but not very often.

When other children came to our house, Miranda would watch them and laugh at them but she was always pleased when they went home. She would join in children's games occasionally but very cautiously and only if we encouraged her. She did not like other children to be too close to her or to hold her hand when playing a circle game like ring-a-roses.

If she was very upset (usually because of other children being noisy) she would hit her head or sometimes head-butt me. When my friends came to visit, Miranda would demand my attention all the time. She would continually want to be picked-up and cuddled. When they left she would be much happier and leave me alone.

Miranda enjoyed visiting my parent's house. It was familiar and she felt secure there. She liked to play with her grandad and would let him take her shoes and coat off. She did not mind if he picked her up and she would try to talk to him in baby language. He would blow-up balloons to amuse her and then let them go so they whizzed around the room. Her granny made green jelly for Miranda and Zöe when they visited. This was the only dessert that Miranda would eat. On one occasion she ate her own dishful and then helped herself to her grandad's jelly as well. She did not understand it was wrong to eat other people's food.

We noticed Miranda was taking more interest in dolls. When she played with her Duplo dolls she would pick-up them up according to whom was around. For example if her dad and Zöe were around she would play with a man and a girl doll. If her grandparents were here she would play with the grandparent

Duplo characters. If two girls were in the house she would play with two girl dolls. This seemed quite clever but a little strange.

I found that Miranda would play an imagination game if I showed her how to do it first. For example if I combed a dolls hair and put the doll to bed then she would copy me and do it. However, if I asked her to do it she would not understand what I was saying. If I gave her clues she would get muddled and comb her own hair and put herself to bed. This showed me that sometimes she was willing to co-operate if she understood what I wanted. However, there were many occasions when she was not willing to co-operate.

She did not like playing tea-parties with dolls and toy cups and saucers but would play tea-parties with real children and real cups and saucers, after a lot of prompting. She would also be willing to put real children to bed and cover them up with blankets but did not like putting dolls to bed!

Miranda was still very obsessed with doors and liked them to be shut or opened according to her wishes. She would sometimes stand in the doorway between the living room and the kitchen so she could see what was happening on the television and also watch me working. She would hide in the kitchen if she did not like an advert or a TV character.

At our church nursery on Sundays there were three children of Miranda's age. I could not help but compare their progress especially as I worked in the nursery. The other children would all ride on a rocking horse, follow simple actions and listen to stories. They could understand words, point and make gestures, play games and play with each other. Miranda seemed much younger than them, very different and aloof. She was still covering her eyes with her arm to avoid contact with anyone unfamiliar or to avoid hearing any sounds she did not like. She seemed to muddle her ears and eyes in this respect! She became upset very easily if another child cried.

When we blew bubbles she would run around and pop them. She would sit down for a drink at snack-time in the nursery but would object if anyone talked to her or came near her and she would not stay in the nursery without me. I missed most of the church services and activities to be with Miranda and envied the other mothers who could leave their children and go into the meetings. Zöe of course would happily go to the older children's Sunday school groups without me.

When I went shopping in Whitstable I would continually feed Miranda bananas to stop her from screaming. She loved bananas but did not like going shopping. The lady in the greengrocers shop would often give us a free banana because she felt so sorry that Miranda was upset. Most people were kind. When we went to our local supermarket we would give Miranda a bunch of bananas as she went into the shop. She would eat them all the way round as we did our shopping. At the checkout, (we always used the same one), we would hand the lady one banana and about five banana skins. She would weigh the banana and estimate the value of the bunch that Miranda had eaten. Even if this seemed an unusual thing to do, the supermarket staff agreed with us that it was better to keep Miranda quiet while we did the shopping than having her scream around the shop!

Miranda had strong preferences for the colours yellow and green. She would bring me yellow clothes to put on. She played with yellow toys and crayons. She loved ducks and of course bananas! When we went out she liked to touch the yellow garages of houses we passed. If there was no yellow around she would gravitate towards all things green.

One day I made the mistake of taking Miranda to the hairdresser shop with me when I had a haircut. Miranda was horrified that someone should alter my hairstyle. She screamed so much that the receptionist could not hear the phone. People walked by and looked alarmed at all the noise. After that experience I changed to a hairdresser who cut our hair at home.

Miranda's speech was coming along slowly. By the end of summer 1991, she could say: "No, Oh dear, Tired, Daddy, Mama, Car, Door, Duck, Tortoise, Hello, Yes and Kissy". There were also a few words which she did not say but she understood. These were: "Eyes, Nose, Mouth, Tongue, Hair, Jump, Shut, Socks, Shoes, Zöe, Elephant, Stairs, Ball, Bubbles, Biscuit, Granny, Nappy and Sneeze". Rudi and I realised we needed to encourage Miranda to speak when she wanted something. If I just handed her what she wanted she had no incentive to speak.

One day the little boy I minded came rushing indoors and told me that all the children were hitting Miranda. I rushed into the back garden and saw them. Miranda was laughing and Zöe and her friends were hitting her very hard. When I made them stop they said they were doing it because she liked it. I wondered if Miranda was laughing because she did not know what else to do but her response did not seem normal. After this I watched her all the time when other children came around in case they hurt her but I was very discreet so that I did not hinder any good social interaction! We had played a lot of games like "Farmers in the den" recently where we all "pat the dog" at the end. I made a mental note to check that if we played it again the children did not "pat" too hard.

We went on holiday to Hastings. I seemed to spend a lot of time with Miranda who never let me out of her sight. Zöe seemed to be with Rudi most of the time. I really appreciated the moments that I could go off alone with Zöe and not have Miranda with me. Rudi greatly appreciated the moments that Miranda would play with him and show him some affection. We had a good week with lots of trips out but unfortunately most of the amusement arcades and seafront rides closed because of excessive rainfall. Miranda carried little toy animals with her everywhere which she kept dropping in puddles. We found an indoor adventure playground with a bouncing castle filled with coloured balls for the girls to play in and we also went swimming a few times. On the whole, we had a lovely time and the girls were generally very happy.

Zöe passed her four year development check with flying colours. She was doing everything that a four year old should be doing and more. I was especially pleased that she was the correct height and weight. I had been worried that she was too little.

The playgroup leader at Zöe's Nursery School asked to see me and told me that Zöe's eye problems seemed worse. She felt that Zöe was having problems because of her sight and was not very confident. I felt quite shocked about this as Zöe was always full of fun and very confident at home. She was an extrovert and a born leader. I wondered whether to change her Nursery School.

Zöe was still regularly sick and seemed to have problems with constipation although her diet was good. We were quite worried but the doctor did not seem to think that anything was seriously wrong. When Zöe was sick it upset Miranda and one night she cried "no, no" and put her arms around her. It was sad but also good to see that Miranda was concerned. Usually Miranda did not show any sympathy or understanding when someone was ill.

In August 1991, Zöe had to go into Kent and Canterbury Hospital for an operation on her eye. She was happily playing picnics with her friends in the front garden when the time came to leave for the hospital and was naturally reluctant to go. Until then she had not seemed bothered. Rudi took us all to the hospital in the car and then brought Miranda home while I stayed with Zöe.

When we arrived Zöe was given a bed opposite a boy who was very restless and upset. He would not open his eyes at all. He had just had the operation that Zöe was going to have and I thought she might be upset by him, but she seemed okay. She soon discovered the hospital playroom and had a really good time in there. I felt she was treating her first day in hospital like a holiday. She was not allowed anything to drink or eat after midnight which we thought would be a problem as she always woke-up at night for a drink but she was fine about it and just accepted it as a hospital rule.

The next morning Zöe was given a pre-med to make her feel drowsy. It did not work at all. She just became slightly delirious and upset. She was meant to take all her clothes off and put on a theatre gown but she refused to take her knickers off and got very angry. She refused to get on the hospital trolley and kept saying she wanted to go home. In the end I had to walk her to the theatre and then hold her on my lap while she was anaesthetized. Back on the ward, I was very upset as were the other mothers whose children had gone for operations. I went out for a walk preferring to be miserable alone.

When I came back, Miranda and Rudi had arrived. Miranda was more interested in the toys in the playroom than in me. It was good that she was not clingy towards me for once. I sent Rudi to collect Zöe from the theatre. I could not bear to look at her in case her beautiful face was bruised and puffy. I felt guilty seeing her suffer and not being able to help. As it happened Zöe came back looking as beautiful as ever and sleeping quite peacefully. She slept all day and all evening but woke up most of the night as usual.

On Wednesday Zöe let the nurse take her eye patch off and clean her eye. She opened her eye so the orthoptist could exam it. He said it was good that she was turning her head only 13% instead of 35% to look at things. This meant that her sight was much better. It was too early to tell if she would need another operation.

Zöe came home quite happily and wanted to play with all her friends but was still very tired and fell asleep in the afternoon. We were thankful the operation was over. Within a couple of days things seemed back to normal.

I regularly took the children to Whitstable to do some shopping. It was a performance travelling by bus with two children and a pushchair especially as Miranda would scream and scream if the bus was late. Sometimes it was twenty minutes late and people at the bus stop would stare at Miranda as if she was a spoilt brat. On one occasion there was a child at the bus stop who suffered from Downs Syndrome. Like Miranda he was crying as he did not like waiting for the bus. Everyone was making a fuss of him and comforting him. A couple of elderly ladies muttered things about how rotten it was to have Downs Syndrome. Miranda screamed and everyone gave us dirty looks - I half expected to be told off because I could not stop her screaming. It was a strange situation. I wanted to say that Miranda was autistic but I did not say anything. She got frustrated very easily and could not cope with the bus being late. I kept quiet; it was too difficult to explain autism to people.

Miranda enjoyed lots of things in life and she did not worry at all about what people thought of her. Did children of two ever worry about things like that anyway or was it just the embarrassed parents who worried? We took the children to a different church one Sunday and it was really quiet there. A lady stood up and said a really long prayer. In the middle of it Miranda decided to wee in her paper nappy. It seemed to go on and on for ages and made a really loud noise. I could feel all eyes turning towards her and I prayed hard that it would not drip out of the nappy edges on to the floor. I was making no progress with Miranda's potty-training.

We took Miranda to the Mary Sheridan Centre for another hearing test. This time Zöe came as well. She was always very good and I felt proud to have her with me. Miranda, on the other hand, screamed "no" at anyone who asked her anything at all. However, the visit was worthwhile as Miranda completely passed this hearing test, despite her best efforts not to. We were told her hearing was fine. The health visitor weighed and measured both children and they were both growing quite normally.

We were told about a type of therapy called "Holding Therapy" and the doctor suggested I try it with Miranda. When she had a major tantrum I was to pick her up and hold her tightly and securely against me until she stopped screaming and calmed down. Apparently this worked well for some mothers and children. Later on, I tried this with Miranda but I soon found that if I held her close to me when she was having a tantrum she was very likely to head-butt me or kick me. However, she did like to be held tight and cuddled by me if she was in a good mood.

The doctor told us about another local family who had a little girl with hardly any speech. We met them and decided to hold mornings of songs and nursery rhymes with the children to try to get them to socialise, to sing and to speak more.

Miranda's tantrums were becoming worse and more frequent. Some days I was lucky if an hour went by without one. Our nerves were bad and we seemed to be forever trying to calm her down. On one occasion, after a really nice afternoon out at Seasalter beach Miranda refused to get into the car to go home. She screamed and screamed so loudly that people came out of their holiday chalets to see what was wrong. Someone asked if she was travel sick or scared of the car. People gave us dirty looks as if we were being cruel to her and muttered under their breath. Eventually we managed to force Miranda into the car and she screamed all the way home.

Meanwhile, Zöe and her friends were growing-up and becoming more resourceful. They found some old beer bottles hidden in a neighbour's house. They collected them up very discreetly and then gathered up a bucketful of rose petals, which they mixed with water and bottled. A lot of people just had thorny bushes with headless flowers left in their gardens.

"We're just playing in each other's front gardens," they told us naïve parents. They had in fact been making bottles of perfume to use on themselves and to sell. I mentioned this to one of our friends who said I should be grateful that the children were only making perfume and not beer.

We lived in a lovely friendly cul-de-sac where the children could play really happily. The gardens were open plan and the children could run from one house to the other. There were lots of pebbles in the middle of our drive, which the children loved to play in – in fact they treated the drive like a beach. We were forever sweeping up stones. Miranda liked to put them down the drain if she had half a chance. I had to watch her constantly. She liked to wander into Zöe's friend's houses but not to play with the other children - she was more interested in exploring everyone's cupboards and putting her hand into my neighbour's fish-tank.

I loved it when Rudi minded Miranda and I could be alone with Zöe. I felt that Miranda was so possessive of me that she was almost trying to push Zöe out. I did not want the close relationship that I had with Zöe to be broken. She was already becoming very independent and had loads of friends. I could tell she was ready for school.

Chapter 3 – Starting School

November 1991 – June 1992

On Zöe's first visit to her future school the headmistress read the children a story about a tiger who came to tea. It was November 1991 and Zöe was just over four and a half. About twenty children sat on big mats on the school floor. I noticed that only two of them were smaller than Zöe.

The children played some ring games and sang songs. Zöe behaved excellently and chose a book to take home called "Downy Duckling" which she proudly put in her plastic school folder. Zöe also bought herself a red school sweatshirt. She was very excited and quite eager to go back again. I was pleased that her first visit was a success.

It was at this time that Rudi and I bought Zöe a new bike. It was a red one called a Raleigh Roller. She was very proud of it and loved to ride around but did seem very accident-prone. She had always been a child who bumped into things and fell over a lot. We presumed this was because she was very active and often played outside. Zöe loved her bike and practiced whenever she could. However, we were slightly worried about her clumsiness.

Zöe was sad to leave her Nursery School but most of her friends there were going to infant school with her, so she would still see them. She made a Christmas book for her Nursery School teacher with pictures and quotes about children and decorated it beautifully. Her teacher was thrilled. When we all said goodbye and left the hall one of the teachers came over to talk to me. She said people at her church would be willing to help with Miranda if ever I needed some help or support. She gave me a very good book about autism. I thought it was wonderful that although my family all went to a Mormon church, which many other religions did not understand or approve of, there was no prejudice against us. Practically every denomination of church in Whitstable had welcomed us at their toddler and playgroups.

Christmas 1991 was coming and two of our closest friends were having a big party. Rudi dressed up as Father Christmas and took Zöe along dressed up as a Christmas angel. They looked fantastic. I was disappointed that we could not all go but Miranda disliked parties and I did not want her to spoil the fun for Rudi and Zöe. There had been too many occasions when we left places early because of Miranda's outbursts and unsociable behaviour so Miranda and I stayed behind at home. This was very slowly becoming a regular pattern. It seemed the easiest option but it was not right.

While I was playing with Miranda I heard the sound of Christmas carols outside. I opened the door and saw the "Lions club" Christmas float coming along our street. (The Lions Club sang carols and collected money for good causes locally). Miranda rushed outside to have a look. Then quite unexpectedly, she climbed up on the float to be with Father Christmas. She loved the carols, the Christmas display and all the Christmas lights. It was good to see her so excited and suddenly the evening seemed magical and everything became so much better. Meanwhile Rudi and Zöe really enjoyed the party.

Zöe was very sick again but the doctor still did not seem worried. She was ill a lot of the time and cried if we went out in the cold weather. This was very unlike her; Zöe had always been such a happy child. There were lots of Christmas parties going on for the children and we went to them by taxi to avoid cold waits at bus stops.

Rudi played Father Christmas at our church party. Miranda was quite amused by this and we wondered what she thought but of course she could not say. Zöe believed there was a real Father Christmas and that her dad and everyone else who dressed-up as Father Christmases were just helping the real one. She drew a picture of what she wanted for Christmas and posted it to the real Father Christmas. She asked for a Kinder egg cat, a Bugs Bunny toy and a ball. My parents minded the children whilst Rudi and I went in search of a Bugs Bunny. They were hard to find but we got a very small one in the end. On Christmas Eve we hung up two stockings. We left out food and drink for the reindeers and left the patio doors slightly open as we did not have a chimney for Father Christmas to climb down.

Miranda was hot and feverish all night and very sick early on Christmas morning. We all went downstairs and Zöe opened all her presents whilst Miranda slept. Zöe was delighted to have everything that she wanted. Her favourite toys were a very noisy skipping teddy and a drum. Miranda's favourite toys were two small rabbits. They were cake decorations but just the right size to hold in her little fingers.

My family all came round to see us on Christmas Day and played with Zöe. I was busy with Miranda who was feverish and delirious. She continued to be ill for the whole of Christmas week and so we ended the year by taking her to the doctor again. I was pleased to see the end of 1991. It had been a year with too much illness.

I took the children to McDonalds in the school holidays and Miranda got me into trouble by eating other people's chips. Whilst I was being served at the counter she headed for the nearest table. She moved very quickly, reached out and grabbed a few French fries. I was very apologetic and embarrassed. I could not take my eyes off Miranda for even a few seconds.

It was getting more difficult to control Miranda when we were out. If a place was too crowded or we heard another child scream, she would have really bad tantrums. She calmed down when she was alone with me in a peaceful and quiet atmosphere.

I had problems with Miranda in some of the shops. At one newsagent the staff especially disapproved of her. They would make comments as I walked around and say "don't let her touch that" and "keep her away from the sweets." I had her on short reins and she was under control. I felt they were unnecessarily rude.

At our little local shop the staff knew Miranda and were always kind to us. They understood if she threw herself on the floor and screamed because another child was crying.

Lots of the children, who lived in our road, came to play on New Year's Day. They helped to make a birthday cake for Rudi. It started off as a piano-shaped cake but ended up as a log. Everyone took turns to help Rudi blow the candles out and we sang "Happy Birthday" numerous times. I hoped we had not blown too many germs onto his cake! Miranda was fascinated by the candles and wanted to grab them. She was over her illness and in a very good mood.

Zöe started school officially on January 13th 1992, a couple of months before her fifth birthday. At first she went for just mornings. She was very excited about her first morning and told me that lots of her friends were in the same class. They had played in a large toy house with a kitchen and she had done painting and music. She was very proud because her teacher told her that she had a pretty dress. Zöe liked to dress-up. She had worn her favourite hair decoration which was a ribbon with a "My Little Pony" picture. She said she thought that she was the teacher's favourite! There were two guinea pigs called "Bubble and Squeak" at school and Zöe was allowed to feed them. We started saving bits of lettuce and carrots for them both.

The problems with Miranda continued and she screamed nearly every day when I took Zöe to school. This was awful for Zöe and naturally upset me as well. Zöe's best friend had also started school and her mother offered to take Zöe in the mornings by car. This worked out well and was much less stressful. I still met Zöe at dinnertimes as I felt it was my duty as her mother to be there. I would arrive at the school with Miranda screaming in the double buggy, which was embarrassing.

Zöe was usually very tired after half a day at school and the walk home was often too much for her so she would sit in the buggy with Miranda. When February came, Zöe was meant to come home from school for her lunch and then go back to school again in the afternoon. This was a problem as we lived a long way from the school. A lot of the time Zöe and Miranda would fall asleep at home and Zöe would be too tired to go back to school again.

One day when Zöe was at school Miranda stood quietly next to me in the kitchen and cried but this time it was not a tantrum. I wondered what was wrong. She cried silently, with real tears and it was very worrying. I missed Zöe not being around in the mornings and I wondered if Miranda missed her as well. Zöe settled quickly at school and made lots of friends. Her friends all seemed much more grown-up now they were at school. When they came to play it was with Zöe and usually not with Miranda. Their games were often too complicated for her to join in. Miranda would usually keep out of their way but sometimes liked to watch them.

We bought a red sleigh which all the children loved including Miranda. We found it worked indoors on the carpet and on the grass outside as well as on the rare occasions when it snowed. My carpet was quite hard-wearing which was just as well. Before we had the sleigh the children had turned our small corner table upside-down and used it as a sleigh so they were delighted to have a real one. Miranda would happily let anyone pull her along on the sleigh. We very quickly made a rule that our stairs could not be used as a mountain slope.

I often took Miranda shopping in the mornings. One day we waited at the bus-stop to catch the bus into Canterbury. A bus went passed going in the other direction and Miranda started to scream. She could not understand why the bus had not stopped and why we were not on it. One bus was the same as another to Miranda. The screaming continued for ages and as usual I apologised for her to all the people at the bus stop. When we got on the bus Miranda was crying and before we got to Canterbury she had started hitting me and throwing herself at the bus windows much to the alarm of the other passengers. I decided to get off the bus early and walk down the hill to Canterbury. The bus driver was taking a detour around the university before going into the main town and I knew Miranda would be even more upset by the detour. I pushed her buggy down the hill towards the town and she fought to get out. I tried to bribe her with bananas but this did not work. A few minutes later the bus we had been on, pulled up beside us.

The driver opened the bus doors and called out: "Do you need any help love? You can get back on the bus again, if you want to."

People like the bus driver who cared made the days a lot better. I really appreciated all the people who tried to help me rather than being generally disapproving of my parenting skills.

By the time I reached Canterbury, Miranda had worn herself out and I was able to do the shopping in peace with her asleep in the pushchair. This seemed to be a common pattern. The tantrums and screaming exhausted Miranda. Sometimes I also felt that sleep was her way of retreating from a frustrating and noisy world.

Just before Miranda's third birthday she said "Zöe" for the first time. We were all very excited. Zöe, who was often tired, was trying to sleep on the sofa under a blanket and Miranda wanted to lie down with her. She said "Zöe" three times to get her to respond. Zöe did respond by pushing her away! Despite this, Zöe was very proud that Miranda had at last learnt to say her name.

Miranda and I visited the Mary Sheridan Centre playgroup in Canterbury. It was a playgroup for children with special needs. I met the playgroup leader and she just let Miranda wander around the room. Miranda did some painting on a large easel using two brushes - one in each hand. She chose her favourite colours, which were still green and yellow. As well as painting a picture she painted her hair, her shoes, her clothes, the floor and the playgroup leader's shoe whilst we were talking. The paint was washable. All the time she was painting she still managed to hold the little toys she carried between her fingers. She never liked to put them down.

Miranda was going to attend this playgroup every Wednesday and I could go there with her. When I took Miranda for the second time, it was different. This time there were five other children and five other mothers. Miranda clung to me crying the whole time. The other children seemed happy to be there. They could speak and seemed to understand a lot more than Miranda. Most of the children had physical disabilities and developmental disabilities.

Gradually Miranda got used to going to the playgroup. The children sang nursery rhymes and there were lots of group activities and stories. Miranda sat through the stories with her eyes open but I had the feeling that her mind had gone to sleep. There was one activity where the playgroup leader would pick up a shape, for example a red triangle and the children had to choose the same. Miranda did not seem to understand this activity at all.

The speech therapist at The Mary Sheridan Centre was excellent but she spoke so clearly that I wanted to giggle. I found myself speaking less clearly and muddling up my words because I was so conscious of how words should be said. Miranda was more interested in the large trees outside the window than in the speech therapy. I was told that she was a very visual child. The staff at the Mary Sheridan Centre playgroup said they would probably try to use simple sign language with Miranda. I was shown how to teach Miranda the word "look". To show her something I would point from my eyes to the object and say "look" and also from Miranda's eyes to the object and say "look." If Miranda wanted something I was to take her finger and make her point to what she wanted. This was to give her the idea of pointing. I was also to try to teach Miranda to say "hello" when people arrived and "goodbye" when they went. Miranda used to say "hello" but seemed to have lost the ability or desire to say it. I came home with lots of ideas about speaking slowly, simply and clearly to Miranda.

I was shown how to teach her to sort out objects. For example if there were two dishes- one containing spoons and one containing toy bricks, I had to teach her to put spoons with the other spoons and bricks with the other bricks. I was not quite sure why I needed to teach her to sort but it would be another good skill to have I supposed.

Miranda and I went to the Mary Sheridan Centre on a little white bus, which came to our house. It stopped to pick-up various children on the way from a few of the villages around Canterbury. Miranda loved the ride there and back. We went on a playgroup outing to a farm in Blean. Lots of people with children sat around on the grass having picnics. Miranda hardly ate anything these days, except cheese quavers or chips. Her diet had become worse and worse. A picnic did not impress her and instead of sitting down she wanted to run around on the grass. I was scared she would trample on someone's sandwiches. She was overjoyed when a tractor arrived and we were all given rides around the farm. She loved the tractor and wanted to go for rides on it over and over again.

Unfortunately she took a dislike to the little girl sitting next to her and hit her in the face. I smacked Miranda's hand and said "no" because she had hurt the little girl. Then Miranda hit me. She kept trying to hit me all the way around the field on the tractor. I was aware of various playgroup leaders, health visitors and social workers sitting nearby and wondered if they would say anything to me about hitting. They kept quiet.

At home one day, when we went out and left Miranda with our friend Pauline, she walked from room to room saying "Where are you?" This was her first sentence. She was upset because we had gone to Tesco and left her behind. This sentence was a one-off. Often Miranda would learn a word or phrase, say it once and then never use it again. However, she used the word "Bye" regularly. When people came she would say it over and over again, in hope that they would go and she also said it when they left and after they had gone.

Meanwhile, Zöe was very happy at school. Rudi and I took her to a dance which we all thoroughly enjoyed. A Caribbean-style steel band entertained us and Zöe danced for several hours with all her friends. She was five years old on March 28th. We put-up decorations, cooked lots of party food and tied five balloons to the front door. Miranda had been good whilst we were getting the party ready except for pulling a bowl full of green jelly out of the fridge onto the floor in her eagerness to have some.

At 12 noon twenty-five children arrived. This seemed rather a lot of children but Zöe could not decide which friends to leave out. Miranda screamed at this intrusion and Rudi took her away. They missed the whole of the party which was a great pity but Zöe and her friends had a wonderful time and Zöe was pleased that Miranda had not disrupted her special day. We played musical statues, musical bumps, pass the parcel and all the usual party games. It seemed much easier to keep twenty-five children happy than to deal with just one Miranda I thought.

The following day was Mother's Day and my parents, sister and her husband came for tea. Miranda stayed upstairs and cried herself to sleep. Even four visitors at once seemed too much for her. I was exhausted and dreaded anyone else coming to visit as I hated seeing Miranda upset.

We did not have a birthday party when Miranda was three years old as it was clear by this time that she really would not want one. Instead because Miranda liked birds so much Rudi took us all to Wingham bird park. Miranda followed the peacocks around even when they went through bushes and under trees. She loved their long tails. I stayed close by to make sure she did not tread on one by mistake. She liked the green ducks as well and would have followed them into the water if we had let her but we made her stay on dry land! The birds were quite tame and did not mind Miranda at all. We had never seen her so happy. Zöe was excited when the birds ate seed from her hand and it was an excellent day out.

In April 1992 my sister and her husband had a baby and named him Joel. Zöe was very excited to have a cousin in England and looked forward to playing with him. Her other cousins lived far away in south-west France.

All through the Easter holidays Zöe and her friends played at each other's houses. Miranda cried whenever the front door opened and they came in or went out of our house. She made it quite clear that she did not like friends coming to play. There was no easy solution to this. It would not have been fair to stop Zöe from playing with her friends and I would not have done that. I felt it was good for Miranda to mix with other children even if she disliked doing so. When it was too cold to play outside, I would often have a house full of Zöe's friends.

We visited a playground at the Sunset Caravan Park a lot. Zöe enjoyed the swings especially one in the shape of a large monkey. I always had to watch Miranda as she would run into swings, go underneath the see-saw and stand at the end of the slide. I was forever running after her and keeping her safe. We were more relaxed in my parent's back garden where Miranda could run about safely and not get into any trouble. Zöe loved to water their plants and climb my parent's apple tree.

Zöe had her first swimming lesson. I sent in a note for the teacher to say that Zöe was very adventurous. She thought she could swim but in fact she was unable to – she was just over-confident. I asked them to watch her carefully. However her teacher did not open the note until after swimming. She sent me back a letter in the afternoon to say that Zöe had jumped into the deep end of the pool and another teacher had to go in and fish her out.

Zöe passed her school medical and developmental check with flying colours. When I went to the school to fetch her for the medical she was in the swimming pool. I watched her from a distance and could see her trying to impress all the boys by saying "look I can drink the swimming pool" and pretending to drink the water from it. They were trying to impress her by ducking under the water.

Meanwhile, I talked to the Mary Sheridan playgroup leader about Miranda and she told me that I should try and get her "statemented" which meant the education authority would have to give her special help with her education. She told me that she thought Miranda would probably have to go to a special school, maybe the local autism unit in the grounds of Zöe's school.

I phoned the autism unit and asked if I could put Miranda's name down as she might need to go there. They told me that they knew about Miranda already but they could not promise a place. It would be up to the education authority and us to decide where she went to school nearer the time. I asked the school for advice on how to handle Miranda's tantrums. I was told to ignore them as much as possible and to try to make sure that she was in a safe place and we were in a safe place when she was having one. Miranda would bang her head, hit or kick if she felt angry or frustrated. I would leave her in the front room, which was safe, and close the door until I thought she had calmed down. Fortunately, Miranda rarely hit other children. She would usually hit family members or adults she knew well.

Miranda had developed a habit of only walking in people's gardens when I took her out. She refused to walk on the pavement and I felt a little worried about this and wondered how long this phase would last. Miranda was very careful to avoid people's flowers and would only tread on the edge of their grass or paths. I wondered if she liked the greenness of the front lawns. If I pulled her back onto the pavement she would refuse to walk, sit down or simply go back on to the green grass again. We lived on an open-plan estate and knew most of the people around. Not many people objected to Miranda walking along the edge of their grass.

Going out was becoming more and more difficult with Miranda. If I took her out in the pushchair she would often throw herself out of it or put her feet down on the pavement. If I did not take the pushchair she was harder to control, running off anywhere she wanted or refusing to move at all. I put reins on her occasionally but lots of people seemed to think that was cruel. I was constantly checking that she had all the little toys with her that she carried around firmly in her hands because if she lost one I knew she would be inconsolable. She very rarely put down any of the little toys, especially her "Little Quints" dolls. These five little dolls had big blue eyes and blonde hair. She loved them.

Miranda liked to take the same route every time we went anywhere and did not like any changes. If we walked passed a bus stop she would scream because she expected me to stop and wait for a bus. She usually liked bus rides. If we did have a bus ride and the bus stopped at traffic lights she would scream because she did not like the bus stopping. She hated it if a bus or car reversed as in her mind they were only meant to go forwards.

Zöe asked me if our neighbour could bring her home from school as well as taking her there. She was fed-up with Miranda screaming and having tantrums outside her classroom in the afternoon. Some of the time Miranda screamed because she wanted to go into the school swimming pool. Other times it was because of all the children at the school. A lot of the time we did not know what caused her tantrums.

Zöe was very happy at school. She enjoyed reading and loved learning. I had lots of good reports about her. I started to read her my old Enid Blyton books and she enjoyed all my favourite stories. Her teacher told her she was the gem of the class and Zöe was very pleased. At parents evening we were told that Zöe was very clever and mature for her age. She was also very confident and a little cheeky. On one occasion my friend from Texas had sent Zöe a beautiful American dress through the post. She was very excited and decided to wear it to school. Zöe took a note in for her teacher saying that she was a new little girl from America who had come to join the class. Her teacher was obviously very fond of her and we knew that Zöe would miss her when she changed classes in September.

Chapter 4 – To France and Back

July 1992 – December 1992

Taking Miranda on holiday to meet French relatives was not a good idea but we did not realise that before we took her to Bordeaux to meet Rudi's family. We went to France in July 1992 and we stayed at a very nice flat where Rudi's brother usually lived with his family. Miranda was puzzled because a flat was so different from a house. She had the most dreadful tantrum as soon as we arrived. She was worried by the language sounding so different and by the unfamiliar surroundings. Rudi had a very large family and Miranda had about sixteen cousins who wanted to meet us. Miranda wanted us to be alone and could not cope – she was very anxious.

Miranda slept about four hours that night and we were all tired and stressed. Sleep was a problem throughout the holiday even more so than usual. She would not sleep for long in strange surroundings. She preferred to stay awake most of the night and then fall asleep the next day in the car where she felt secure. I spent most nights sitting up with her in the flat and watching Babar the Elephant videos. This was the only way to keep her quiet and I did not want her to scream. We were four floors up, in a block of flats where no-one knew us and the other residents would probably not appreciate their sleep being disrupted.

Miranda's diet was still limited to a few foods. She refused to eat most things. We could not find any oven chips in France and the crisps we found were different to the ones she had in England so she would not eat them. We ended-up going to McDonalds for French Fries twice a day. Zöe was pleased about this as she collected Happy Meal toys.

Over the next few days the children met all their French cousins and we visited most of Rudi's relatives. Miranda was so unhappy about socialising that I wished I had stayed at home in

England with her. Zöe, on the other hand, was very excited. She had made lots of new cousins and the language barrier was not a problem for Zöe or her cousins. Fun and play were the same in any language. The weather was hot and we had a glorious day at Rudi's sister's house in the country. We had lunch outside and the children played most of the day in their paddling pools or rode around the garden on toy tractors. At another house the family had a hammock tied between the trees and a rope swing. It was wonderful to be outdoors so much. Most of all it was great to see how well Zöe adapted to being in France and how she loved playing and eating outside with her many cousins.

Miranda was very upset in Bordeaux and would head-butt, hit and kick me every couple of hours. She did not like the tall apartment blocks where we were staying or the different noises. The sound of the lifts, the creaking of doors and the chatter of voices outside all alarmed her. When we took Miranda anywhere built-up she refused to leave her pushchair. Everything was too strange for her and I wondered if she realised she was on holiday or if she thought we had taken her away from her home permanently. She was very, very angry.

On the second week of our holiday we decided to have a break from all our relatives. We drove through the pine forest areas to Arcachon. We climbed over the high sand dunes and walked down to sea. It was wonderful for the children to see a beach that was so long and sandy. Zöe loved the soft sand and buried us in it. She giggled at first when she saw a few naked people on the beach but after a few minutes the novelty wore off. No-one worried about whether you wore clothes or not. It was a different way of life here and the beaches were a huge contrast to the cold pebbly ones of Whitstable.

For the first time in months, Miranda dropped the little dolls which she carried everywhere and ran as fast as she could along the edge of the sea. She was really excited and so relieved to be away from all our friends and relatives. She just wanted to be free and run as far as possible. We took turns to chase after her so she did not get lost. She ran and ran and ran, laughing with joy. It was wonderful to see.

The following day we decided to avoid people again and Rudi drove through the pine forests to Sanguinet where we found a shallow lake among the trees. We paddled for ages in beautiful clear water. Then we went on to Biscarosse where the lake was so big that it was like the sea. Zöe and Miranda were really happy and played for ages in the water. We had an excellent day and Miranda cried real, silent tears when we had to return to the flat. She liked us all to be alone and outdoors.

On our final night in the Bordeaux area some well-meaning friends decided to take us out for a meal. This was a bad idea because Miranda hated sitting down with people and did not eat proper meals. She started moaning so I took her for a walk while the others sat down and ate. We walked a long way and without realising it walked into an area where we were not allowed. Three security guards in uniforms stopped us and wanted us to go with them somewhere. I wondered if we were being arrested. My French language skills were not very good so I did not understand what they were saying. Miranda saved the day by screaming as loudly as she could for what seemed a very long time. The security guards took pity on us and let us go! Meanwhile Zöe and Rudi enjoyed their meal without us.

I was relieved to leave Bordeaux as I felt that it had all been too much for Miranda and me! However, I was very pleased that we had made the effort to go there and that Zöe had met all her French cousins and experienced a different way of life. On the way back to Northern France we stayed in a small hotel again. This time the people in the room next to ours complained that our children were too noisy so at 10 p.m we took the girls on a long car ride to the seaside town of Berck. We hoped they would fall asleep.

They stayed wide-awake but it did not matter because we had a wonderful last night in France. The town was bustling with holidaymakers, shops and restaurants were open and there were bright lights everywhere. Zöe went on the largest carousel that we had ever seen. It was brightly lit-up and overlooked the beach and sea. When we eventually got back to the hotel, the girls slept well but Rudi and I were awake a lot. I was too tense to sleep in case Miranda woke-up and made a noise.

The next morning the French holiday season seemed to be in full swing and the beaches were crowded. Lifeguards patrolled the beach warning people not to go in swimming as the sea was too rough. We saw a child being rescued who went out too far and we watched another lifeguard in a dinghy giving rides back to the beach to various children in trouble. Zöe and Miranda played happily in the puddles of water away from the sea and Miranda made her first sandcastle, with our help.

We journeyed on to Le Touquet where we were all impressed by the large detached houses, the trees and the prosperity of the area. The beach there was very quiet and uncrowded. Zöe had chosen a toy for her cousin Joel and she buried it in the sand before running away to play. She could not remember where it was and we spent a lot of the morning searching for it by digging up various parts of the beach. We never did find his toy so we had to buy him another one.

Rudi and I could not believe how good the children were. Miranda was well-behaved all day. We spent a long time in a children's play area at Boulogne and then had an uneventful crossing on the ferry home. It was good to be back in England and we vowed never to take Miranda to the south of France to visit relatives again.

We had brought an enormous paddling pool back from France and whenever the weather was warm we filled it up and Zöe's friends came in to play. Some days we had as many as ten children in the back garden and pool. Miranda liked to watch them all splashing around but usually kept her distance.

Occasionally we would leave Miranda with our friend Pauline and take just Zöe out. We took her out for a meal at a pub with a bouncing castle, to Margate beach and amusement arcades, to children's play areas and to many other places. It seemed very strange not to have Miranda with us but we were all so much more relaxed without her there. Zöe had been rude to us lately and she had told us it was because she was jealous of Miranda and all the attention she was getting. My parents took Zöe and one of her friends for a special treat to "Farming World" nearby. Our neighbours took Zöe to the beach with them and to the swimming pool. Everyone decided to make more fuss of her.

Zöe loved it at weekends when Rudi would take her out to practice riding her bicycle. She found balancing difficult and still needed the stabilisers but we were proud of how well she was doing. I felt bad when I remembered that at one time Zöe and I had been really close but now Miranda was taking up so much of my time that I was not able to do as much with Zöe. Miranda always clung to me and objected if I gave her to Rudi or to anyone else. It was good to be needed but I felt needed too much.

We were all fed-up with Miranda's behaviour. We had tried shutting her in the bedroom for a while when she was aggressive. It did not do any good. She would come out of the room just as angry as when she went in it. No discipline worked at all and I was bruised from being kicked and head-butted. She seemed to need to have the tantrums and nothing was going to stop her. Sometimes I closed all the windows so no-one outside could hear Miranda. I was ashamed that Miranda screamed so loudly for no apparent reason and frightened that someone might think we were doing something to her. Fortunately, we had quite an open house policy and knew all our neighbours well. They were all very supportive and accepting of Miranda. I was still worried that someone might walk-by and report all the screaming coming from my house. Various health visitors had introduced me to other mothers whose small children had problems but all the other children I met could talk a little and only had mild learning difficulties so it made me feel even more despondent. I was yet to meet a more difficult child than Miranda. I was trying hard with her but felt I was failing.

I phoned the mothers of some other autistic children that I had heard about. One lady told me that she always had holidays alone and her husband minded their child. Her husband had separate holidays too. It was much too stressful to take their child anywhere different and they had no friends who would look after him. He could not cope with strange people or unfamiliar places. Another mother told me that she never had visitors or people around for meals as it made her son too anxious. I wondered if eventually our social life and holidays would come to an end. I hoped not - we did not want to give in and wrap our lives around Miranda.

My mother told me about a club called "Contacts" for children with various problems. I phoned the organiser and she told me that they regularly had swimming sessions at the school swimming pool. The lady who ran the club had worked for many years with autistic children and was very helpful. She arranged for Zöe, Miranda and me to be taken to the swimming pool and for a helper to look after Zöe and play with her so I could concentrate on Miranda. Both children loved the water and were very happy with this arrangement. Miranda liked to jump into water from the side of the pool. She would not put down the little toys she carried and I had to be careful that she did not lose them. When we got out of the swimming pool Miranda screamed as she wanted to stay longer. She head-butted me, hit Zöe and was angry all the way home. Later I phoned the lady in charge and apologised for Miranda's behaviour. She told me that she thought Miranda was quite severely autistic but she said we were always welcome at the "Contacts" club. It was good to have somewhere to go where I felt that the children would be accepted and understood. I looked forward to taking the girls there to relax and splash around in the water.

The "Contacts" club had an outing to Brambles Wildlife Park. Zöe would not sit near us on the coach as Miranda kept hitting her. She decided to sit with the other friends she had made. She loved the animals at Brambles especially the rabbits. Miranda loved the blue and green budgerigars best but the outing ended with tears and tantrums as usual. We were there for too long as far as Miranda was concerned and she wanted to go home. An elderly lady tried to calm her down.

I said, "It's no good. She doesn't understand what you are saying."

"She may not understand the words," the lady told me, "but she'll understand the tone of my voice and that I'm being kind to her." I thought this was an interesting comment. Sure enough Miranda calmed down when the lady kept talking to her very quietly.

Most of the children who came to play at our house were very good but of course all children can be naughty. One six year old girl turned out Zöe's wardrobe and tried on all her dresses then left them in a pile on the floor. Others would come in and raid the cupboards for biscuits and crisps while I was busy with Miranda. One day I found Zöe and her friends colouring in my front door step with felt-tip pens. Fortunately they used washable ones.

However, none of these children were as naughty as the boy who took Miranda's doll. The pebbles in our front drive were still very popular with Zöe and her friends. One day the children had scattered stones all over the road and pavement so I went outside with a broom and swept them up. I took Miranda with me so that I could see what she was doing. She ran around quite happily and then she tripped and dropped her favourite little doll. It was a blonde-haired tiny doll with green knickers, from her set of "Little Quints" dolls. She had carried this particular doll around for months and it had been all the way to France and back with her. She took it with her to bed and held it in the swimming pool and everywhere else.

A gang of boys were playing nearby and one of them grabbed her little doll and ran down the street with it in his hand. Miranda immediately followed him screaming. I chased after them but I was too slow. The boy dropped her little doll down the drain at the end of our road. Miranda ran up to the boy and opened his hands to get her doll back. I asked him why he had thrown it down the drain but he denied doing it and blamed the other two boys who were standing nearby. I was very angry and Miranda was inconsolable.

We tried to get the drain cover off but it was too heavy. Word soon spread among the children in the street. They all knew who the guilty boy was and banned him from their games. He was not a local child. A little girl knocked with one of her dolls that looked similar to Miranda's and offered to give it to her. It was a kind thought but Miranda knew each of her dolls individually and the new doll looked too different. When Rudi came home he managed to lift-up the heavy drain cover and remove Miranda's doll from the water. I disinfected it and gave it back to her. The objects, which Miranda held seemed to be more precious to her than real people.

I decided that I needed to try something different to help Miranda. A neighbour had given me a newspaper cutting about Cranial Osteopathy and how it could help children with autism. There was a Cranial Osteopath in Canterbury, a few miles away so I took Miranda to see him. The Osteopath asked me various questions about Miranda. He said he felt the treatment would only help if there was something physically wrong with her body or head that could be put right by gentle manipulation. I laid Miranda down on a bed and he gently massaged the back of her head and the bottom of her spine for about ten minutes. She screamed all the time as she did not like being made to lie down and she did not like being touched. He was very kind and gentle with Miranda but afterwards he told me that he would definitely not be willing to treat her again. I found the whole experience stressful because Miranda was so upset.

We rushed to get the bus in the pouring rain and managed to get the bus driver to stop just as he was pulling away. He was abrupt and rude to us. Miranda was still screaming and I was very upset. I cried on the bus all the way back to Whitstable. A couple of ladies came over to see what was wrong which made me feel worse. I had a terrible migraine by the time we arrived home and Miranda had worn herself out by screaming. We both went to bed and slept all the afternoon. My parents both looked exhausted when they brought Zöe home in the evening. She had slept overnight at their house and been with them all day. She was very excited about it and longed to go there to sleep again.

The school holidays ended and Zöe went back to school. She had been eager to see all the friends she had at school who did not live in our street. Miranda's first day, without me, at The Mary Sheridan Centre playgroup arrived. I tried to tell her she was going there but she did not understand what I was saying. She was happily watching a video when the minibus arrived and was not at all pleased when she realised she was being taken away. I handed Miranda over screaming and the playgroup leader promised to phone me when they arrived.

"There's no easy way to do this. I'll just take her," she said. I watched the minibus driving away and felt guilty for abandoning her. I had a phone call soon after to say she had arrived safely and not to worry. It was wonderful to be able to go out on my own at last. I wanted to run along the beach nearby and shout out "I'm free" even if it was only for a few hours.

Miranda came back home just after lunchtime. She had enjoyed the minibus ride both ways but had not enjoyed being at playgroup. She had slept there when she first arrived and then had woken-up and cried. She went from one helper to another putting her arms up and wanting to be cuddled. When she came home Miranda was very happy to see me and good all afternoon.

The next visit to playgroup was much better. Miranda had cried on arrival but then settled down and painted a lovely picture with lots of coloured stripes. Zöe and I were not sure if it was a sunset, worms or a maze. Only Miranda knew and she could not tell us. On her third visit Miranda went horse-riding and apparently she enjoyed it.

Meanwhile, Zöe kept coming home from school with accident forms. On one occasion she had a bump the size of an egg and a note to say her head had been bleeding. I took her to the Health Centre but she seemed fine. Her friends also seemed to have various knocks and bruises but I was worried that Zöe seemed to fall over far more than them. A few days later Zöe came home very drowsy. She had hurt her head in the school playground whilst playing. My neighbour had collected her from school and carried her to the car. Zöe had concussion and I was worried - I phoned for a taxi and took her straight to the Health Centre again.

Miranda was screaming so much that at first everyone thought she was the one who was hurt. The doctor called an ambulance for Zöe and my parents came and took Miranda to their house. I went to the local hospital casualty unit with Zöe. We were there nearly all the evening and by the time we saw a doctor Zöe was fully conscious and alert again. I kept her away from school the next day and we had a quiet day at home playing with toys. Zöe seemed fine and back to her normal self. She told me how impressed she was by the chocolate dispenser machine in the hospital and asked if she could have one at home so she could put coins in and have chocolate whenever she wanted.

Zöe had another eye test and she was unable to read the bottom three lines of the chart again. Her schoolwork was very good though, so no further treatment was planned for the time being. I wondered if her poor eyesight was causing her clumsiness. At school the teacher said that Zöe's work was fine and she was a "bright little poppet." I was pleased that her eyesight was not affecting her work. It did not seem to be a serious issue at that time.

Miranda regularly brought me her coat and shoes when she wanted to go out. She would lead me to the place where she wanted to go. Usually this would be across the fields near our house to the food shop. Miranda rather liked the Noddy collection box on the counter and tried to buy it a few times. She would usually put bananas, jelly babies and bubbles in my shopping basket. When we arrived home I would blow bubbles for her to pop. She would eat the bananas. The jelly babies were like little dolls and she would play with them for ages. She liked the green ones best. Miranda did not eat the jelly babies but other children did when Miranda was not looking. Zöe also loved being outside and she would collect snails and slugs in a bucket of leaves and tell me that they were her pets. She also loved going blackberry picking with all her friends.

In the mornings we watched "The Big Breakfast" on Channel 4. Both children liked the cheeriness, good humour and the bright colours in the programme. On Thursday 29th October they announced that they were going to be filming in Whitstable. Zöe was very excited and wanted to be on TV so at 8 a.m. Rudi took us to Woodlawn Street where one of the presenters was door-knocking. Then Rudi went back home and videoed the programme for us. Zöe, did her best to be in view of the television camera. I followed her around with Miranda in the pushchair who seemed to sense that something exciting was happening. When we came home we watched the video and saw ourselves among the crowd on the Big Breakfast Show. We appeared on the show three times and Zöe asked all her friends to come round so that she could show them how famous we were!

We took the girls shopping and Miranda chose more "Little Quint" dolls. It meant that she had twenty-five of these tiny dolls now. She always chose the ones with blonde hair and blue eyes. She carried little dolls everywhere and when she was in the bath she held them up high out of the water so they did not get wet. Rudi often swung her around in the evening as she loved this game. Only then would she let go of her dolls so that she could hold both of his hands. Zöe chose a Little Mermaid doll at the shops. She liked to have all the latest toys and the ones that were popular at school.

Half-term ended with another accident. This time it was in Whitstable High Street and Zöe fell flat on her face. She did not use her hands to save herself and banged her head again on the concrete. Rudi picked her up and Zöe fell asleep within ten minutes. She slept for about an hour and then seemed her normal self. We kept her close to us all the weekend in case of any bad effects after the fall. We were extremely worried but she seemed completely fine and went back to school quite happily the following Monday.

However, Zöe was getting a lot of headaches and would be sick every couple of weeks and we were not sure why. As a child I had suffered from migraine and been very sickly so we presumed she was suffering from a form of childhood migraine. She seemed fine in between her headaches. She was a very active child and always out playing or trying new things.

Miranda seemed quite healthy apart from having eczema. However, she had developed a very strange walk which she did when she had a tantrum. Her knees seemed to bend the wrong way as if inverted and I worried that she would break her legs. My mother wondered if she had rickets and friends wondered if she was double-jointed. She would also click her bones. I mentioned it to several health officials but no-one seemed very worried. I was told that children's legs were more flexible when they were little.

Miranda's diet was also a problem. She would only eat chips, crisps, bananas, biscuits, crackers, butterscotch dessert, green jelly and chicken nuggets. She would not eat anything else at all, ever. People found that hard to believe or accept and often she was given sweets as a present. I asked a dietician if Miranda's self-imposed diet could be causing damage to her bones or her legs but the dietician did not seem worried about it.

I found that if Miranda was upset, I could sometimes calm her down by drawing lots of pictures of little dolls and ducks. She loved to watch people drawing. She would not usually draw by herself but one day she drew me a picture of a duck. It was very good but unfortunately it was on a Magna-Doodle screen so I could not keep it but took a photo of it. Later I told her that I loved her and she drew me a heart. I think it was a heart and not a misshapen duck. Zöe meanwhile was producing the most marvellous artwork and we were really proud of her. She seemed to be good at everything.

My mother minded Miranda so that I could go and see Zöe in a Christmas play at her school. I felt very proud when she came and sat on my lap. Zöe loved Christmas and we went to lots of bazaars in December and enjoyed seeing Father Christmas. Before going anywhere, Rudi and I would have to judge how Miranda was going to react. If she was likely to scream, head-butt or make Zöe miserable then we would not take Miranda with us. However, we still took her to our church every week as we had lots of friends there who had known us all for years. It was good when we could all go out as a family.

Miranda had a playgroup Christmas party and I was invited but I knew that if I went along Miranda would be cross because she expected me to be at home while she was at playgroup. She did not like me to be "in the wrong place" - that was the way her mind worked. I decided not to go because I could not face being at her playgroup and seeing Miranda angry and having tantrums. When Miranda came home from the party she was very happy and laughed a lot. She had received a beautiful fluffy duck as a Christmas present and had enjoyed her morning.

The same day, Zöe came home from school with two of her friends. They put on a video to watch and immediately Miranda's mood changed for the worse. It was a video that Miranda particularly liked about Pingu the penguin. We tried putting on different videos but she still moaned. It seemed that she liked watching videos of her own choice when she was alone but she did not like any videos that other people chose. We tried having music on instead of videos. The same thing happened. If Miranda chose the music and we put it on she would be fine but if someone else put the music on (even if it was a song she liked) Miranda would object and try to turn it off.

School finished and Christmas holidays began. The children loved the Christmas decorations so we put them up quite early. I took them out Christmas shopping and told them they could choose a Christmas present. Zöe wanted a box of fifty Christmas crackers. They were the same price as a doll. She cleverly worked out that she would get fifty presents from inside the crackers and fifty hats for herself and all of her friends. They spent hours pulling the crackers and making them bang. A box of Christmas crackers was much more exciting than a conventional toy! Miranda liked big colourful toys with lots of small figures inside. We bought her a "Big Red Fun Bus" and a yellow aeroplane for Christmas. Zöe wanted a "Glow in the Dark Boglin." It was an ugly rubbery monster face with a mouth that moved and big eyes. Boglins were so popular that I could not find one in Whitstable or Canterbury. Rudi went to Hamleys in London especially to buy one for Zöe. There was a bomb scare that night and Hamleys was sealed off. We all wondered why he was late home.

Two days before Christmas, Zöe had another fall. We were just walking along the pavement and she fell heavily again. We were worried about her and wondered why she was so clumsy. We sensed that something was wrong but did not know what to do. I felt sorry for her and bought her an enormous old metal rocking horse that she kept looking at in the window of a second-hand shop. It was painted white and gold and we called it "Merry" as in "Merry Christmas." All the children loved it.

We took Zöe to an optician in Canterbury to have her eyes tested again. They put drops in and checked her sight. They said she was slightly long-sighted and might need another operation but glasses would not help. Zöe was very good throughout the examination and did not seem very worried about her eyes at all.

We had an excellent Christmas Day. No-one was ill. Both children were happy and loved all their presents. Zöe especially loved a little shopping trolley with lots of plastic food inside. Rudi relaxed, cooked us Christmas dinner and played lots of music while the children played. It was the most wonderful Christmas and I felt full of hope for the future.

The Contacts holiday club gave Zöe an enormous Bugs Bunny to look after. They told her they had nowhere to store it. It was about six foot long and she had become very attached to it during the summer holidays. Our house was being taken over by toys but if it made the children happy then life was easier for Rudi and me. We finished the year by going to the Contacts Christmas Party. I sat and drew Miranda lots of pictures to keep her calm while Zöe joined in the games. Then a children's entertainer called "Colin the Clown" came to entertain everyone. Zöe and Miranda both loved him. He did tricks with a dove and a rabbit then made balloon animals. I was pleased we had made Miranda stay at the party. It was worth it because she enjoyed watching the clown so much.

1992 ended happily. Zöe and I blew feathered hooters at each other and laughed while Miranda raced around. I wondered what changes 1993 would bring. It was just as well that none of us had any idea of what lay ahead.

Chapter 5 – Dreadful News about Zöe

January 1993 – April 1993

Zöe did not seem well but it was hard to pinpoint the exact problem. Most days she would wake-up with a tummy-ache or headache. In January 1993 we took her back to the hospital eye clinic for a routine check. We were told that she still had a slight squint but would not need another operation unless it became worse. She started back at school but did not seem to be as bright and cheerful as usual despite doing well there and having lots of friends. She had a nosebleed which was unusual and was still being sick about once a fortnight for no apparent reason.

Zöe had hurt her head yet again when some children knocked her over at church. She seemed to recover very quickly from her various mishaps but even so, I decided to take her to the doctor again. I saw a student doctor as our family doctor was away and explained that every few days she would have a tummy-ache or a headache and occasionally would be sick. I said she was quite clumsy too. He checked Zöe over but said that she seemed fine physically and that constipation could cause headaches and tummy aches. He suggested giving her more high fibre foods and syrup of figs.

I did not feel that this would be a lot of help but followed his advice anyway. At home between school and playing with her friends Zöe seemed to be lying about a lot and resting. Occasionally in the night she would wake-up frightened or would kick and twitch in her sleep.

In February my parents took Zöe to Herne Bay and she walked along the sea wall and fell off. Her squint seemed to be getting worse rapidly and she was becoming even clumsier. I phoned and made an appointment with the school doctor again just in case he could give me any advice about all Zöe's problems. I wanted her coordination checked thoroughly. I made another appointment for the eye clinic as well.

One of Zöe's friends came for lunch and they were happily laughing and eating tomato soup. Then Zöe said, "I feel sick" and was sick back into her soup. The other little girl looked horrified and pushed her soup away.

This was just one occasion that stuck in my mind when Zöe seemed healthy one moment and sick the next. Between bouts of illness Zöe went to birthday parties and school as usual. Friends were still coming and going every day when she was at home. Miranda would sometimes watch them play and sometimes disappear upstairs to play alone. It snowed at the end of February and both children enjoyed the snow. Miranda was upset when I kept getting snowflakes in my hair and kept wiping my hair with a paper towel. She hated anything to be different about me.

I took Zöe to see the school doctor again on March 4th. He checked her over and also did some tests to see if she was dyspraxic. He said she seemed okay and I felt reassured a little but at home I felt uneasy still as Zöe was not her usual self. She seemed discontent and restless despite having lots of friends and plenty of toys to play with. We tried to give her more attention to compensate for Miranda taking up so much of our time.

On March 16th Zöe was sent home from school. She had a very bad headache and was sick again. The teacher told me how sorry they all felt for Zöe as she seemed so little and had been crying because of her headache. I phoned a doctor who said the problem was probably constipation again and prescribed a laxative. After a few days I sent Zöe back to school as she seemed to be better and wanted to see all her friends again. Her teacher told me that Zöe had said to all her friends that she was "complicated" and that was why she was not at school. We all agreed that she was complicated as well as having been constipated.

March 21st was Mothering Sunday and both children made me pretty cards. Zöe was sick again and had another headache but she seemed to recover well. Miranda also seemed to be having a bad week and was aggressive towards me.

On March 25th I went to see the doctor again. I told him that Zöe still did not seem well and he arranged to get her an urgent eye appointment at Canterbury hospital. He also asked me for a urine sample from her. He gave me some medicine to help Miranda sleep so we could all rest more and he checked Miranda's clicky legs for me. He said she was deliberately stretching her joints too much but there was nothing we could do about her. She only did it when she was in a temper and she would probably grow out of the habit.

It was Zöe's 6th birthday on Sunday March 28th. We held her birthday party the day before. As usual, Zöe wanted lots of her friends to come. Thirty children seemed a lot now as they were all getting bigger so we decided to have two parties with half the children coming to each one. Zöe chose a cake from our cake decorating video and Rudi made it for her. It was in the shape of mushroom house and he decorated it with lots of little marzipan animals and flowers.

When Zöe came downstairs she had a tummy-ache and a headache but at the thought of her birthday parties the symptoms seemed to disappear. She wore a beautiful white sailor dress with blue trimmings, which she had chosen from the front cover of a catalogue. She looked beautiful with her roundish baby-doll face, sparkling eyes, cheeky smile and shoulder length brown hair which never seemed to grow quick enough for Zöe. She was a pretty, bright and bubbly six year old and we felt very proud of her.

Miranda enjoyed watching us move the chairs around. We had to work out how to fit everyone into the room. At dinnertime, Pauline came to take Miranda out. We knew that Miranda would object to lots of people coming to our house so it was best if she was not there. We wanted Zöe to have a special day and to enjoy herself.

The dinnertime party went well. Most of the children who came lived in our road and they were relaxed and happy. They still all played regularly outside together and went to each other's houses after school. We played musical bumps, pass the parcel, and all the usual games indoors and in the garden. There were no fights, no sulks and no spilt drinks. They were all growing up into lovely children.

Miranda came back from her outing smiling and happy. Rudi and I busily prepared everything for the second party at 4 o'clock whilst Zöe played outside. It was not long before she came in crying because she had fallen over and grazed her knees. She rested a while and then went out to play again. The children for the next party arrived. They were mostly girls from her school this time, aged five to seven. They were full of fun and mischief and kept us on our toes. They were not interested in party games but wanted to play with Zöe's toys. They were far more energetic than the children at the dinnertime party and we felt worn out. My sister Olive arrived to help, with cousin Joel who was nearly one year old. We had decided to let Miranda stay with us during Zöe's second party but were ready to send her away at the first sign of disruptive behaviour. As it happened this time Miranda was angelic and interested in everything that was going on.

The next day was Sunday, Zöe's actual 6th birthday. We had bought her a Pogo stick but because she was so accident-prone decided to hide it until she was older. She was delighted with the red and yellow scooter we gave her instead. At church Zöe usually went with the older children for singing and Sunday school lessons but today she did not seem well so I kept her with me whilst I helped to run the nursery for the little ones. We did all the usual activities: Play-Doh, drawing, nursery rhymes and singing. There were nine children in the nursery. Miranda was really aggressive towards me, head-banging and hitting again. It was too noisy for her. At least she had been good yesterday at the party, when it mattered the most.

On Monday, Rudi went back to work as usual and Olive took Zöe and me to Canterbury Hospital eye clinic. Our doctor had made an emergency appointment for us because Zöe's eye had deteriorated so quickly. We arrived at the eye clinic hospital for our 1.30 appointment and could see that we would have a very long wait. We saw an orthoptist who was very concerned about Zöe's squint. She asked about her general health and I told her about the sickness and the headaches.

Then we had another long wait and saw the specialist. He seemed very worried about Zöe as well and said he wanted to do a much more thorough examination. He gave us the choice of waiting until he had seen all his patients or coming back another day. We decided to wait. Olive took little Joel to the hospital shop and bought us all something to eat. I phoned my parents and said we would be a long time. They were minding Miranda and I was worried that she would be giving them a hard time but she was being good.

We waited over four hours at the hospital. Zöe never complained about the long wait or the nasty eye drops put into her eyes. However, she was feeling very hot and I worried that she would be sick. I went to the hospital shop and bought her a cool sundress to change into and gave her lots of drinks to cool her down. The hospital playroom only had a few old furry toys inside so I bought her a toy golf set and we played golf whilst we waited! Zöe had been given a toy dog for her birthday. Its mouth opened when you pressed its tummy. I would throw the golf ball and Zöe would make the dog catch it. Soon a few more children joined in and this made our wait more interesting. Outpatients was a boring place for children.

Zöe was struggling to keep awake by the time we managed to see the specialist again. He told us that Zöe's eye should not have turned inwards as suddenly as it had. He did not know why it had happened but said that possibly something was wrong behind the eye. He said we would have to make an appointment and see the head paediatrician. He sounded very worried.

The next day Zöe was sick again and her headache seemed worse. I kept her at home and phoned the school. The headmistress told me that Zöe was very happy at school and doing well there but she felt that something was physically wrong with Zöe although she did not know what. I phoned the doctor and he told me to lower her temperature with paracetamol and to send another urine sample down to the health centre to be tested. The sample turned out to be clear. My parents came to see Zöe but she was too ill to play with them and just lay on the settee all day.

On Wednesday morning I called the doctor again. Zöe had been ill all night and I felt she was dehydrating with fever. I had the windows open to cool her down and was giving her loads of fluid. A different doctor came and said that she would have to go to hospital if she did not improve. He told me to phone the Health Centre again, in a couple of hours. One of my neighbours took a prescription to the chemist for me. She said she would mind Miranda if Zöe was rushed to hospital suddenly.

I phoned Rudi and he came home from work in London. I phoned the health centre twice more and asked for a doctor to call again. The receptionist said one would be coming soon. Zöe's temperature was extremely high and she seemed delirious. At one point she did not seem to recognise us at all. By 5 p.m. we were feeling desperate and about to take Zöe to hospital ourselves without any referral from a doctor. Then at last, a doctor turned-up. We had not seen him before but he recognised Zöe's symptoms and told us to take her straight to Canterbury Hospital Children's Ward. Later we found out that he had treated another little girl with the same illness.

We quickly packed a suitcase and went. Zöe perked-up and she seemed well on the journey to the hospital. I stayed there with her and Rudi took Miranda home.

It was March 31st, my sister's birthday. Olive cut short her celebrations and rushed to the hospital to see Zöe. Only four days before we had all watched Zöe having a great time at her parties and it seemed almost unbelievable that she was in hospital now. Various doctors and students came to see Zöe and did tests on her. They were especially concerned with her motor nerves. They were worried about her left leg and her lack of balance. At last they seemed to be connecting her symptoms together. The headaches, sickness, falls, her tiredness and the eye slipping. One of the student doctors told me that she thought Zöe might have a bruised brain but she was not sure. Zöe was good the whole evening and did not seem to mind all the tests she was having. She was very eager to go to the large hospital playroom. I felt relieved that at last doctors were trying to find out what was wrong with her.

Zöe slept badly and was sick again on Thursday morning. She hated taking her medicine but apart from that she was handling her visit to hospital well. The doctors did some blood tests, a urine test and they x-rayed Zöe's head. All the results showed nothing. Zöe felt a lot better and wanted to go home as soon as possible. The ward was noisy and crowded at night with lots of admissions and children crying. I slept with Zöe in her bed. Nobody seemed to mind.

At 3 a.m. on Friday morning I woke-up and started to read a copy of the Readers Digest. An article caught my eye about a Dr Epstein in New York and his amazing brain surgery. I felt slightly uneasy when I read the symptoms of a brain tumour. They were similar to Zöe's symptoms. I put the article to the back of my mind. I was sure Zöe would be okay and we would soon be home.

When Zöe woke-up she went to play in the hospital playroom. She seemed her bright bubbly self again and was running around happily. The time came to give Zöe a brain scan. She was very good and stayed very still while the machine took photos of her brain. We laughed and said it was like putting her head in a big washing machine. When we arrived back on the ward a nurse told us that someone would come and see us in five minutes with the results.

The ward seemed to empty of nurses and doctors. A man who was not a member of the hospital staff came over and talked to us and said he expected that Zöe had childhood migraine. He seemed to know a lot about medicine. I carried on playing with Zöe and promised her that we would go and buy a special helium balloon from the hospital shop soon. More than five minutes passed and no-one came to see us. I could see a crowd of doctors and nurses at the end of the ward talking and I felt uneasy.

Eventually a man came over. I had seen him before and thought that he was a paediatrician. He asked to see me alone. A nurse offered to mind Zöe while I followed him to a room a long way off where he introduced me to a clinical counsellor. It was there that he told me the most terrible news. Zöe had a brain tumour. It was malignant, cancerous and on the brain stem, which affects all body parts both mental and physical. He said that things did not look hopeful but Zöe would be sent to Guy's Hospital in London at 4 o'clock that afternoon and then go to the Maudsley Hospital. I was in a state of total shock and could not believe it. I asked how long she had to live if she did not recover and he said about a year. I told him about the doctor in New York whom I had read about in the Readers Digest and how he performs operations on brain tumours but he did not seem hopeful.

I felt faint as though I was floating and everything seemed unreal. The clinical counsellor kept offering me tea. I did not drink tea and it was the last thing I wanted. I phoned Rudi. He said he would leave Miranda with my parents and then come to the hospital. Then I phoned my sister and our friend, Pauline. They all came to the hospital as soon as they could. Rudi and I made it clear to everyone that we did not want Zöe to be upset or to know how seriously ill she was – everyone had to be positive.

I wanted to get back to Zöe in the playroom and buy her the balloon that I had promised her. I saw one of her little friends there. She was in for a minor operation and would be going home soon. I quietly told her mother about Zöe and she was upset. I took Zöe to the hospital shop and bought her the balloon I had promised her.

Another of my friends from church was in hospital waiting for her baby to be born. Our church believed in giving blessings to people to hopefully heal them. Rudi and her husband prayed together and laid their hands on Zöe's head to bless her. Then her husband said the words, which he felt inspired to say. The blessing confirmed my worst fears. He did not bless her that she would get better but said that angels would look after her and she would not be forgotten. I prayed silently that if Zöe was going to die, it would be peacefully and she would not suffer.

We went back to the hospital ward. Miranda's health visitor was there by chance. (A few nights before I had dreamed that I was talking to her in a hospital but of course at that time had no idea that all this would happen). She wanted to talk to me but I did not want to talk to her or anyone else. Apparently another child from the Mary Sheridan Centre also had a brother or sister in a London Hospital. I remembered someone saying to me that you could not have two children with serious health problems because life could not be that unfair. I wondered who had said that and thought how it was so wrong. I wanted to be left with Zöe so we could carry on playing. A doctor wanted me to look at her brain scan but I did not want to see the tumour that might kill her. I wanted the medical staff to go away. I felt I was in the middle of a nightmare and everything seemed unreal.

Zöe said that she wanted to go to the London hospital with her daddy and not with me. She was angry with me because she could not go home. We said that doctors were going to try and help her headaches to go away. Rudi told Zöe that a special car was going to take them both to London. The health visitor was worried that I was not going with Zöe as well but Zöe made it very clear that she wanted to be with just Rudi. It was hard for anyone to understand how close Zöe and Rudi were because I was always looking after Miranda. I felt guilty about all the time I had spent with Miranda rather than Zöe.

I kept trying to pack Zöe's bags and empty out the hospital locker but I seemed to be doing it in slow motion and just sat on the hospital bed not achieving much. I said goodbye to Zöe and Rudi. There was a rail strike and the roads to London were busy. I knew that Rudi was in shock and I was pleased that he did not have to drive there in his own car with Zöe. Our hearts were breaking and it all seemed unreal.

My sister and I went to collect Miranda from my parent's bungalow. They were very upset and we decided to keep quiet about how seriously ill Zöe was until we knew more. I was worried my parents would not cope with the news that Zöe could die. They were very fond of her and Zöe loved going to see them.

Miranda was very pleased to see me and hummed "Head, Shoulders, Knees and Toes." She gave me lots of hugs. I felt mean because I knew I would be leaving her again in the morning and going to London. When we arrived home, all the neighbours were waiting outside our house to see us and ask about Zöe. They offered help and wished her well. Everyone was shocked that Zöe was seriously ill – especially the staff at Zöe's school.

I spent the evening tidying up the house. I felt I had to keep busy and keep working in hope that there would be no time to think. The phone kept ringing as the news spread that Zöe was going to Guy's Hospital. She had hundreds of friends and everyone was concerned.

I went to bed with Miranda and cuddled her to sleep. She had been very good whilst Zöe and I were away. I was so shocked and worried that I did not sleep at all. I went downstairs and sorted out cupboards all night. Keith, my brother-in-law, came at 6 a.m. to drive me to Zöe in London and Pauline came to look after Miranda who was still asleep in bed.

When I arrived at Guy's Hospital, Rudi told me that we were going to the Maudsley Hospital at 9 a.m. They specialised in brain operations. The Maudsley only had a tiny playroom and we sat in there with Zöe trying to keep her amused. She made it very clear that she only wanted to be with Rudi and resented me because I had kept phoning the doctors when she was ill. She thought it was my fault that she was in hospital. Lots of different doctors came to do tests on Zöe and check her balance and her vision. She did not mind that but she hated having more blood tests.

The doctors told us that Zöe had "hydrocephalus" which I understood to mean "water on the brain." The brain tumour was blocking the flow of brain fluid and the blockage was making Zöe's eye go inward and her face-shape change. The tests the doctors had done also showed that her speech had deteriorated slightly and her left leg was affected which was why she seemed clumsy. The headaches, sickness, tiredness and constipation were all caused by the tumour. They warned me that her personality could change as well depending on how the tumour grew.

We asked about the cause of her brain tumour. We had been to Bulgaria on holiday during the Chernobyl nuclear power disaster and soon after I had become pregnant. I wondered if the radiation had affected us and in turn Zöe. We wondered also whether a knock on the head could cause a brain tumour – Zöe had banged her head a lot over the years. There were no clear answers.

At 2 o'clock Zöe had to go to the operating theatre. She was upset that she had to undress and wear a theatre gown but otherwise was very brave. The doctors and nurses were kind and let her keep her clothes on until she was too unconscious to care. The surgeon told us he would shave off as little of her hair as possible so she would not feel self-conscious. He would keep Zöe's cut hair for us and give it back to us later in case we wanted to keep it.

Rudi and I went to the hospital canteen as there was nowhere else for us to go. Our mouths were very dry and we could hardly talk. We were too shocked and much too anxious to eat anything.

After Zöe left the operating theatre she went to Intensive Care and to the Recovery Room. She had two dressings covering her cuts and stitches. One was on her head and one on her stomach. A shunt had been inserted which was to drain the excess fluid from her brain and relieve the pressure. She was wired-up to a machine which monitored her heart-beat, pulse and temperature and had a drip inserted in her hand and an oxygen mask on her face. She was in a lot of pain because of the wound on her stomach and the painkillers seemed to take a long time to work. She was semi-conscious from 4 p.m. to 9 p.m. when the staff took her back to the main ward. Rudi just sat and held Zöe's hand all the time. He did not want to read or do anything except be with Zöe. I just wanted to keep busy and phoned all the people waiting to hear news of her.

I went to see the surgeon who had done the operation. We had met him before and he was interested to know that we belonged to the "Mormon" church. He told us that he had been on a skiing holiday in Salt Lake City where our church headquarters were. While he was out there he had an accident and was treated by a Mormon doctor. The doctor waived the fee as he told the surgeon that when he was in England on a church mission he had received free medical treatment, so he wanted to return the favour.

He told me that sometimes when a shunt is inserted there are problems of infection and blockages. Zöe's brain fluid would drain down into the gut and would be urinated out. Her tumour was very deep down and could not be surgically removed. I asked him how long Zöe had to live.
He hesitated and I asked, "A year?"
He said, "No less than that, maybe just a few months."

I told him about the Readers Digest article and about Doctor Epstein, in New York who removed difficult brain tumours. I asked if he could help. The surgeon said that he had consulted with him before about other difficult cases and if I wished he could ask for a second opinion for us regarding Zöe. I asked him to send Zöe's files etc out to Dr.Epstein and said we would pay any costs to do that. He agreed but he told me that he believed the tumour was in much too dangerous a place to remove. However, radiotherapy treatment could shrivel it a little giving Zöe slightly more time.

The surgeon explained a lot to me but I was so shocked when he said that Zöe might only have a few months to live, that by the time I returned to Rudi, I could hardly remember anything he had said.

Rudi and I decided not to tell people how low Zöe's chances of recovery seemed to be. We did not want Zöe to know that her disease was life-threatening. Why make her worry when she was usually such a happy, sunny child? We wanted her to carry on enjoying life as much as she could.

After Zöe came round from the anaesthetic she was moved back onto the main ward. She was pleased to have all the wires taken off but hated having a drip left in. There seemed to be a lot of problems on the ward. There was a shortage of nurses and lots of agency staff, many of whom seemed to be quite harsh with each other. The drip did not seem to work properly and the nurses kept squeezing the tube to make the fluid go through. Every hour a nurse would come and monitor Zöe's eyes, reflexes, temperature and blood pressure. Zöe was cross because she just wanted to sleep.

There was also a problem with ants on the ward. People had been called in to destroy them a little while before but the ants were back. If we left any food or drink on the hospital lockers it would be covered in ants very quickly.

We were told that we could not sleep in the ward near Zöe at night. There was visitors' accommodation upstairs and we were expected to use it. I asked the nurse if one of us could sit in the chair next to Zöe instead of going upstairs to sleep. She agreed to this, so I sat by Zöe's bed and Rudi went upstairs. Halfway through the night Zöe woke-up and wanted Rudi. I told her I would go and get him and she said she would be fine while I was gone. A nurse was nearby so I was not too worried about leaving her.

When we came back downstairs, Zöe's bed was surrounded by doctors and nurses and there was blood everywhere. As soon as I had gone Zöe had become hysterical. She had torn the drip out and also an elastic band they had left in her hair together with lots of her hair. After that, the staff on the ward agreed that just for one night we could both sit with Zöe and one of us did not have to go and sleep upstairs.

Zöe woke-up feeling very drowsy and irritable. She said she hated hospital and was very bored. At Guy's Hospital and Canterbury Hospital there had been lots for children to do but the Maudsley Hospital seemed to cater more for adults.

At lunchtime we had two visitors from our church who prayed and gave us all more blessings. The sun shone through the window while they visited and we all felt slightly calmer. We hoped for a miracle and believed that God could make Zöe better. One of our friends told us that he felt inspired to ask the whole of our church to visit the Mormon temple and pray for Zöe. (The temple is considered to be a very sacred place). He said that he would arrange it. It would show that we all had faith and maybe a miracle would happen.

We played with Zöe for a while. She was too weak to walk and very subdued. A lot of my family arrived later on in the afternoon which livened-up the quiet hospital and made the day a lot shorter for Zöe. She was very pleased to see everyone. My mother, sister and brother-in-law, aunt and cousin all came with biscuits, fruit and presents. Zöe fancied a McDonald's meal so

Olive went out and bought her one. The day seemed to be improving rapidly.

Night-time came and Rudi decided to stay in the chair next to Zöe's bed. She felt secure with him close by. I spent the night in the visitor's accommodation but cried so much that I hardly slept. I was so worried about Zöe.

The next morning, Zöe played on the ward floor with the boy from the opposite bed. He had a life-threatening brain tumour as well and was due to be transferred to a hospital nearer his home that day. The two of them were playing with some ants they had collected. They had cups with food in the bottom and a magnifying glass. They would catch the ants and watch them feeding. The ants seemed more interesting than the toys in the playroom. A nurse came in and was horrified to see the children playing with them. She told us that important visitors were due to inspect the hospital and we must not let them know that there was an ant problem. We promised we would keep quiet. Hospitals were being closed down too easily for the slightest reasons. After the game of ants finished Zöe and her friend found a new game to play, with medicine syringes. They would fill them with water and squirt plants or people. They thought it was very funny to put the medicine syringes between Zöe' dolls' legs and to make the dolls pretend to wee.

The next morning Zöe was meant to have a CT scan again. She screamed and screamed for over fifteen minutes and no-one could make her lie down to have the scan done. She was sent back to the ward and we tried to think of ways to bribe her. The nursing staff came for her again but she refused to lie down and have the scan. They told us all that unless she co-operated she would have to stay at the Maudsley hospital longer. Zöe said she did not care. They gave Rudi and I fifteen minutes to persuade her to have the scan. There was a Woolworths quite nearby and I told Zöe that if she co-operated I would buy her anything she wanted from it. She agreed to have the scan but only if I bought her a baby Boglin toy.

I had fifteen minutes. I rushed to Woolworths and there was a massive queue, which was never going to go down in fifteen minutes. I picked a baby Boglin toy off the shelf. Then I said to the person at the end of the queue:

"My little girl is in hospital and unless I take her this toy in ten minutes she is refusing to have an important scan. Do you mind if I go in front of you?"

The lady was very kind and agreed. Then she told the next person in the queue who passed on the news about Zöe to all the other people queuing in Woolworths. Everyone wished me good luck with Zöe as I rushed away with the toy. I arrived back at the CT scan area just before the staff were due to leave for the day and Zöe happily let them do the CT scan with the Baby Boglin by her feet.

More visitors came to see Zöe but she refused to talk to them because she was so angry and fed-up. She wanted me to go home and be with Miranda and said all the hospital treatment was my fault. I had called the doctor and he had sent her to hospital, when all she had was a headache. She only wanted Rudi with her because he could give her piggy-backs and carry her around when she felt weak and I was not strong enough.

Olive phoned and said she thought I should come home and see Miranda. I had only been away a few days but Miranda was missing me. Zöe was going back to Guy's hospital the following day and she seemed quite happy about that, so reluctantly I decided to go home and leave Zöe and Rudi again. I hugged them goodbye and went back to Whitstable.

It was strange to go back home but it was lovely to see Miranda again. Pauline had looked after her very well and kept a diary for me of what Miranda did each day. The garden seemed very green and pretty with lots of beautiful daffodils in bloom just like when I had first brought Zöe home from hospital after she was born. Whitstable seemed so pretty compared to London.

All day long people phoned with good wishes and we had loads of letters and get-well cards for Zöe. The most beautiful ones were the hand-made ones from Zöe's friends at school. Friends called in to see me and I felt overwhelmed. Everything in Whitstable seemed very different and the world seemed unreal. My parents were having a hard time coping with the news of Zöe's illness. We were all in shock.

Rudi phoned from Guy's hospital the next day and said Zöe had been given another scan. This time she had gone into a long machine like a tube and her whole body had been scanned. They had injected her and sedated her beforehand but she had taken ages to go to sleep being quite determined not to give in to unconsciousness.

I took Miranda for a walk over the fields to the little shop where I walked so often with the girls, to buy them chocolate Kinder eggs. I told the lady in the shop about Zöe and she was so upset that she could not stop crying. Someone else had to come and serve the customers and I felt really bad that I had told her. I spent ages contacting the people who had written to us. Initially the shock about Zöe had made me feel hyperactive. I had hardly slept for over a week but now I was beginning to feel very tired.

On Thursday 8 April, Rudi and Zöe came home by train from London. It was Easter and Zöe was pleased to be home for a few days. That same evening a big outing had been arranged by our church to the temple where everyone would pray for Zöe and for a miracle to happen. It was very important for Rudi and me to attend. Pauline had arranged to mind Zöe and Miranda and another friend was going to drive us to the temple. It was just over an hour's drive away, in Surrey. We met the rest of our church there and also met a man whose daughter had died the year before of a brain tumour. She was about the same age as Zöe. I felt it was especially kind of him to come and pray with us all.

The temple ceremony went well but just as it was finishing there was a phone call asking us to go home. Zöe was very upset and calling for us. We all sat in silence in the car afraid that Zöe would die before we reached home. Ever since she had been diagnosed we lived in fear that she would die suddenly. We hated leaving her even though we had the most wonderful babysitter.

When we arrived home Zöe was sleeping peacefully. She had been extremely upset during the evening and complained of toothache. Miranda had also been crying because she hated to see Zöe in tears. Zöe's granny had called in to see the children and she had been upset too. I felt very sorry for Pauline and we both felt guilty that we had gone out. I felt annoyed with our church and especially with God. Where was he? He certainly did not seem to be looking after Zöe.

The next day was Good Friday. Rudi and I were exhausted but Zöe seemed quite well and cheerful when she woke-up. In the morning, five of her friends came to play. They watched Mr Bean videos and had a good laugh. In the afternoon, we took Miranda and Zöe to Herne Bay park. They had a lovely time on the swings but afterwards Zöe suddenly fell asleep in the car. For a moment Rudi and I thought she had died. We were so relieved when we realised she was breathing and just sleeping peacefully.

At about 6 p.m. Zöe started to complain of toothache. We could see that she had a new tooth coming through so gave her some medicine to relieve any pain and help her to sleep. From 10 p.m. onwards Zöe kept waking-up with very bad nightmares. She seemed half awake and half asleep. She kept walking about and saying to us "my body is dying, I've lost my spirit and I've lost my shadow." It was terrifying and we kept reassuring her, saying that it was okay, we were here and she must not worry. She did not seem to recognise us and kept running around the house and screaming. She cowered by the radiator shaking. Then Zöe went back to bed but she woke up again and again. Rudi and I were really scared that she was dying and watched her all night.

By the morning Zöe was calm and did not seem to remember what had happened during the night at all.

However, Zöe told me that when she was in hospital and almost unconscious she had heard a nurse saying that she was dying. We told her everyone was doing their very best to try and make her better.

We had to take Zöe to Canterbury Hospital on Saturday morning to have the staples removed from her stomach. They had been put there during her shunt operation. Needless to say, she was not very happy at the prospect of this and Miranda was not very happy either. Zöe screamed at Rudi and the nurse. She tried to run away and was hysterical again. Miranda also became very upset which made matters worse and I had to take her away into the playroom to calm her down. It was another stressful morning. However, we all had a good afternoon with lots of Zöe's friends dropping by to play. Miranda was calmer and played happily by herself.

The next day we went to an early birthday party for their cousin Joel. We celebrated Miranda's birthday at the same time. Joel was going to be one year old on April 17th and Miranda was four years old on April 13th. The party was really good and both the children enjoyed it. Miranda loved an Easter bunny that someone gave her but the highlight of the party was when everyone sang "Happy Birthday" to her and she blew the candles out. Miranda was very excited. Zöe also received quite a few presents from friends and relatives. She especially liked animals and was given lots of fluffy toys. They were beginning to take over the bedroom.

On Easter Monday we took both girls swimming. That was what Zöe wanted to do and we felt that we should put her wishes first now. We had a very good time and all enjoyed ourselves. Zöe seemed lively and did not seem at all worried about her slightly shaven head. Back at home, she did not feel as confident and asked for the stabilisers to be put back on her bicycle so she could play outside. We had intended to put them back anyway.

We watched her playing with her friends. She seemed to live for the moment and not worry about the future. Miranda meanwhile was happy being left alone to play. She was no longer the focus of attention and we were not doing as much therapy with her or making her play. This suited her fine. The actual day of Miranda's 4th birthday went by quietly. She had hardly any presents and no celebrations. We were not sure if she knew that it was her birthday. It did not matter as we had celebrated the weekend before at her little cousin's birthday party.

Chapter 6 – To Ronald McDonald House

April 1993 – July 1993

Zöe was very angry about all the hospital treatment. Who could blame her? Like most six year olds she wanted to play with her friends and have a good time, not be going to hospitals. Rudi took her back to Guy's Hospital for two days after the short Easter break. Zöe needed to have a mask made, to wear on her face during radiotherapy sessions. She was very unhappy about the mask and gave Rudi a hard time. They both came home stressed.

Miranda had stayed at home with me and had been very sick but I kept it quiet and did not tell anyone. I felt that the people around us might think that Miranda had a tumour as well, if I said anything. A couple of friends had already asked me if Miranda could have a tumour because of her autism!

The people at Guy's Hospital had arranged for us all to move up to London that Sunday so we could be together while Zöe went for radiotherapy treatment. We had a bad weekend with both children feeling aggressive and being irritable. We left for Guy's hospital at 4 p.m. This time we took lots of toys and clothes for the girls. We were going to a place called "Ronald McDonald House." It was a building paid for by McDonalds Restaurants where children with life-threatening illnesses could stay with their families whilst having hospital treatment. Different companies sponsored rooms in the house and helped to pay for the running costs and the wonderful facilities.

Before Ronald McDonald house had been built, families had been divided with one parent sleeping at the hospital ward with their sick child and the other parent at home miles away with other children.

The journey from Whitstable to London Bridge was about 60 miles. Miranda especially liked the ride, which was just as well since we would be going from London to Whitstable and back most weekends for a while. She laughed if we went fast and especially liked it when we overtook anything. A lady from Zöe's school gave us a cassette tape of children's television theme tunes and we played it over and over again in the car.

Ronald McDonald House was quite modern and built-up around a beautiful little garden and courtyard. There were family rooms with four beds inside and windows with a view of the garden. There were lounges, quiet rooms, a large airy kitchen and the most marvellous playroom with lots of toys. To Miranda's delight there were also television rooms where we could watch children's videos. It was a splendid place, better than any hotel that we had ever seen.

Nevertheless I was nervous about how Miranda would react in a place where everything was so different and of course we were all worried about Zöe. Guy's Hospital was just across the road. In every family room there was a telephone so that the hospital could get in touch with patients at any time. Rudi took Zöe over to the children's hospital ward to have a test for tuberculosis – we were told there is a type which can cause tumours. While they were gone Miranda and I explored Ronald McDonald House and we loved it. It was very peaceful and quiet despite being so near to London Bridge. Both children slept very well that night. It was lovely to wake-up and hear the birds singing in the little garden outside our windows.

The next day Rudi took Zöe to St.Thomas's hospital for a fitting of her radiotherapy mask. I had wanted to go as well but could not take Miranda. She could not keep quiet or still for long, especially in a hospital. We could have left her at home with Pauline for a month but we wanted our family to be together in London. Zöe continued to make it very clear that she wanted to be with Rudi and not with me or Miranda but I was hoping this was a passing phase and she would soon feel more favourable towards us later. When Rudi and Zoe returned we went to St.James Park to feed the ducks an activity that we all enjoyed.

Rudi worked for British Telecom in London and he could walk from Ronald McDonald House to his office. His colleagues were fundraising for us in case Zöe needed to go to New York for an operation. They were constantly in touch with us all and had all sorts of events planned to raise money. I kept the girls with me most days while Rudi was at work but Rudi took time off when necessary.

We took the girls to Rudi's office to meet everyone and they enjoyed their visit. Miranda loved the canteen, which had green cushions and green chairs, still her favourite colour. She raced round and round with excitement. Zöe drew pictures for everyone on large pieces of scrap paper. She was an excellent artist and pleased to be busy. It was a good morning out!

Ronald McDonald House was full of families who had very ill children. We made friends with two more families who had boys with brain tumours. We had lots to discuss and compared any ideas or new treatments we heard about. It was good for us all to talk and we all tried to help each other. There were other children at the house who had heart and kidney problems. Some were waiting for transplants. Most families had travelled a long way to London for treatment.

Many people worked at Ronald McDonald House voluntarily. Miranda particularly liked an elderly man who mopped the floors and she was eager to help him. The bucket of water was a big attraction. She also wanted to help the gardener with the weeding. She was very interested in her new surroundings and did not seem afraid. In fact, Miranda was so totally unaware of all the illness and suffering around her that quite often she was a joy to be with. Zöe and Miranda enjoyed racing around the little circular garden at Ronald McDonald House. Zöe would go very fast on roller skates and Miranda would try to catch her!

I always watched Miranda very carefully when we went across the road to the hospital wards in case she touched any medical equipment or climbed onto a child's bed but she was generally very good.

Zöe had started her radiotherapy treatment which was usually once a day. At first Zöe was scared, bad-tempered and uncooperative. One particularly bad day stayed in my mind when Zöe was very tired. Her appointment was at 4 p.m. and she had been sleeping all afternoon. We woke her up and Rudi went ahead with her to the radiotherapy waiting room. I followed with Miranda in the pushchair. When we arrived there Zöe was sitting on a chair holding on to Rudi and crying. She shouted at Miranda and me and told us to go away. She looked at me as if she hated me and glared at Miranda.

"I don't want you here," she screamed, "especially her."

Miranda was upset because Zöe was crying and I walked away in floods of tears. A nurse stopped me and asked what was wrong. I explained that my other daughter was having radiotherapy and this daughter was autistic. She was upset so I was taking her for a walk to calm her down.

I pushed Miranda to the River Thames and stood on the middle of a bridge looking down at the water. For a moment, I wished we were dead and at the bottom of the river. Miranda was screaming and screaming. She did not understand why she was in London or what was going on and she hated seeing Zöe upset. Zöe was angry because she was going through so much. The treatment probably would not work and she would die anyway. Rudi was heartbroken because he was so devoted to Zöe. It seemed that life was not worth living.

I pushed Miranda very quickly away from the bridge. Hundreds of commuters were rushing towards us, on the way to London Bridge station to catch a train. Just a few years ago, I had worked in London and commuted there by train every day. I had never dreamed then what a nightmare life would become. There was nowhere quiet enough to go, no peaceful places where I could just be alone and manage to avoid people. I took Miranda to a small swing park but the slides and swings were covered in broken glass. I did not want to take Miranda back to the hospital or Ronald McDonald House so we kept walking. After a while we arrived at St.Paul's Cathedral and I telephoned Rudi to tell him where we were.

When Miranda and I arrived back at Ronald McDonald House Zöe apologised and said she did not want us to go away and she would be good in future when she went to radiotherapy. I told her that lots of people paid money to lie on a sunbed and have light shone on them because they wanted to have a suntan. They wore special goggles to protect their eyes. Was it that different wearing a mask and having rays shone on you to make you better? (I knew it was a lot different but Zöe did not). Zöe said she would lie on the radiotherapy bed and pretend she was sunbathing next time. From then on Zöe was good when she went for her treatment and a lot calmer. Miranda and I went with her to the radiotherapy room daily. Rudi came as well when he was not at work.

Between radiotherapy sessions and when Rudi was not working we could take the girls out and about together. We had two pushchairs with us as both girls needed one. Zöe became tired easily and her legs were a little wobbly. Miranda was easier to control in a pushchair because if she was walking she would not always go in the same direction as the rest of us and might wander into the road. We took the girls to the Elephant and Castle shops, which were within walking distance and to the HMS Belfast, only a few minutes away. We found a little park near Bermondsey Village Hall with the most beautiful blossom trees. There were swings and climbing frames for the children to play on and we bought a kite to fly.

We also took the girls to lots of toy shops and on outings further away. We travelled mostly by tube or train and soon got to know what stations to avoid because of all the steps. Steps were difficult with pushchairs and children. We also tried to avoid travelling in the rush hours. We often went to Hamleys in central London. Miranda would always choose the same toys there: "Little Quints" and Sylvanian Family yellow ducks. Zöe bought herself a Viking suit and hat! We found a shop near London Bridge where they sold Kinder eggs with tiny terrapins inside, which the girls collected.

Most days we took Miranda to McDonalds. By now, she only ate fries, quavers, crisps, plain biscuits, cream crackers and very occasionally green jelly. Over the last two years she had refused more and more foods. Zöe loved the Happy Meals with all the toys inside the boxes at McDonalds. She still ate lots of fruit and vegetables and had a generally healthy diet.

We had a weekend back in Whitstable and saw all our friends and my parents. Zöe's teachers and school-helpers came to visit her at home. It was hard to believe that only a few weeks ago Zöe had been going to school every day. Zöe managed to fit a lot into her weekend and even went to a birthday party and on a bouncy castle. She was very tired afterwards and we were exhausted too.

When we went back to Ronald McDonald House we had lots of visitors. One friend brought her five year old daughter to see us. They lived near Wales and had left early in the morning, catching several trains. Zöe was delighted to see her friend and we all went to the nearby park where the children played. Zöe and her friend loved the blossom trees and threw lots of blossom over each other. It was a beautiful day and lovely to see the girls laughing and happy.

Other days were more stressful. One morning, Rudi had gone to work and I was at Ronald McDonald House with both girls. Miranda was having a kicking, hitting and head-butting tantrum, when three visitors turned up. I felt I should be entertaining them or making them a cup of tea at the very least. They had come a long way to see us. However, I had my hands full with Miranda and was about to take Zöe to radiotherapy. Fortunately they were very understanding and could see the situation I was in.

The days seemed long between the radiotherapy treatments. On colder days we would watch videos at Ronald McDonald House or go over to Guy's Hospital children's ward where they had a playroom and a games console. Zöe loved to play "Super Mario" or "Mickey's Quest" games. She would get very frustrated if the games proved too difficult. On warmer days we would go on outings.

One day Rudi and I took the girls to the Natural History Museum which they both enjoyed. Zöe bought a jewel dinosaur keyring and a dinosaur poster. She was fascinated by the dinosaur bones and liked the earthquake simulator there. Unfortunately she cut her finger on the corner of the poster she had bought and got very upset. She was a lot more sensitive since all her hospital treatment had begun. Normally a cut finger would not have bothered her at all. Miranda chose a green fluorescent snake from the museum souvenir shop. She seemed to enjoy our outings and seeing so much of London. I thought of the saying "when you are fed-up with London you are fed-up with life." There was something for everyone in London.

On the way back to London Bridge station Miranda nearly slipped between the train and the platform. Rudi and I were holding her so she was safe but she lost the little ducks she carried with her everywhere. There was also a bomb scare and police vans everywhere. Bombs had exploded in London twice the weekend before.

I was pleased to go back to Whitstable for my birthday on May 2nd. Two of our friends cooked us a meal and brought it round. We saw my family and went to church as usual and Zöe played with all her friends at home. It seemed as if we had two lives now, one in London and one in Whitstable. On the way back to Ronald McDonald House we stopped at a funfair. Zöe never wanted to go back to London – the radiotherapy treatment seemed to make her tired and grumpy.

On Wednesday May 5th Rudi and I had a meeting with the various doctors from Guy's Hospital. The children stayed in the playroom of Ronnie MacKeith Ward with the Play leader. There was a big collection box with a special spiral groove inside and both children loved putting 2p pieces in there. The coins would go round and round for ages before they dropped down. A friend who did nursery rhyme therapy with Miranda, had given us lots of bags of 2p coins and the children spent ages putting them in the collection box one at a time.

At the meeting Rudi and I were told again that Zöe probably had less than a year to live. Her tumour was very big and the doctors were not even sure that the radiotherapy would help. Apparently, some tumours responded well to radiotherapy but some did not. They hoped that the radiotherapy would help the tumour to shrink or slow down its growth but once the radiotherapy stopped, the tumour would grow again. Of course we hoped that the tumour would shrink completely. We wanted a miracle. They told us that Zöe would probably grow more and more tired as time progressed. She would have problems with breathing and chest infections. They said the scans and information about Zöe had been sent to America but they felt the doctors out there would be unable to operate without killing her. Worse still Zöe would only be allowed thirty sessions of radiotherapy otherwise she would suffer more brain damage. There was no good news.

In the afternoon, Rudi and Zöe went to the London Dungeons while Miranda and I went to the chemist to buy nappies and other essentials. In the evening we took them for a ride around the West End of London to see the lights. They both fell asleep in the car. Miranda woke-up when we returned to Ronald McDonald House and I sat downstairs in the kitchen with her until midnight talking to another mother who had also been told that her child had less than a year to live. Miranda objected all the time I talked to anyone so it was hard to have a long serious conversation. She kept kicking me as she wanted me all to herself.

Later that week, Rudi and I took the girls to London Zoo. It was lovely to walk from the tube through Regents Park. We had a wonderful day. Miranda liked the ducks and birds best, especially when they flapped their wings at her and opened their large beaks. She ran after some ducks and fell in a muddy puddle. I took her to a gift shop and bought her some new clothes: a large sweat-shirt which could double-up as a dress and some new socks. Miranda very rarely said anything but when the lady in the shop talked to me, Miranda said to her very loudly, "Shut-up." I explained that she was autistic and had fallen into a large puddle. The lady took us into the backroom and gave me a large towel so I could dry her and put her new clothes on. She also gave Miranda a "toy sample" which she could not sell. It was a beautiful roaring tiger.

Zöe liked the monkeys at the zoo best and laughed a lot when they scratched their bottoms. She also liked the rabbits and the elephants. There was a fairground-style roundabout at the zoo and Zöe wanted a ride. She went round and round, waving to us every time she saw us. The weather was perfect that day and we stopped at a swing park on the way back to the tube station. Sometimes everything seemed so normal that it was hard to believe Zöe was so seriously ill. Later when the photos of her on the roundabout were developed, I was overcome with sadness and felt that she was waving goodbye to us.

In the evenings at Ronald McDonald House, the girls often watched videos. They especially enjoyed The Care Bears. One of the bears was called Cheer Bear. He slid down rainbows and made children feel better. I often watched "The Care Bears" with the girls and could see similarities between Care Bear land and how I imagined Heaven. The Care Bears gave hope to everyone and looked after all the children. They also encouraged positive attitudes and mind over matter. I wondered if Zöe's zest for life and determination to keep going could make her better.

I would answer all the cards and letters we received in the evenings. We had lots of letters from well-meaning friends about miracles and how people recovered from serious illnesses etc. My favourite letters were the ones that talked about normal everyday things and not about illness or religion. I had a letter from a friend who complained about the dry rot in her house.

She went into great detail about how she was trying to decorate and restore an old house to its former glory but everything was going wrong. She wrote with humour and moaned about her children playing up and said how she had piles of ironing to do. It was a good letter because it reminded me that life was still going on outside the hospital environment in much the same way as usual.

My double buggy had broken and someone lent me an old-fashioned double pushchair to take up to London. It meant that if Rudi was working I could take both the children out for a long walk. We often went along the back streets to the Elephant and Castle. A couple of times I had problems with trees. The trees in that area were so wide that I could not get the pushchair passed them. I had to explore the area and look for streets with wide pavements and smaller trees. At the Elephant and Castle we would go to Woolworth and buy small toys, usually a Mini-Boglin monster for Zöe and a little doll for Miranda.

Zöe seemed to get tired in the late afternoon probably because of the radiotherapy and then would be irritable or have a tantrum, which was very much out of character for her. There was a machine in Ronald McDonald House where you could get cups of fresh milk. Zöe loved milk and when it did not work one day she ran out of the house screaming with frustration. On another occasion Rudi and I wanted to take the girls to get some food from the shop around the corner. Zöe was determined not to come with us and was really cross. She picked up a telephone and started to dial 999.

"I'm phoning the police. I'll dial 999. I'll tell the police about you. You can't make me do what you want."
I said to her, "Why don't you dial 666 instead and then a policeman might come standing on his head?"

It was an old joke but she thought it was funny. We gave in on that occasion and Rudi stayed in with Zöe whilst I took Miranda to get the shopping.

Zöe continued to have strange nightmares and sometimes woke-up confused in the night, often screaming. Her hair had started to fall out because of the radiotherapy and we would find chunks of it on the pillows. I was pleased that we all slept in a family room together. We encouraged Zöe to sleep and rest more so she was not overtired but she was determined to live life to the full.

I wanted to spend more time with just Zöe as our family still seemed to be split in two rather a lot: Rudi with Zöe and me with Miranda. Rudi agreed to mind Miranda while I took Zöe to Oxford Street to see the film "Jungle Book." It was lovely to go out with just Zöe. She was so easy to take on the tubes, in the shops and everywhere. I had no bad behaviour, moaning or screaming from Zöe when we were out, unlike my outings with Miranda. Even when Miranda did behave excellently around the shops I was always stressed and anxiously waiting for her next tantrum to occur. With Zöe I could relax much more. She was happy and we had a wonderful afternoon.

When we arrived back we were told that an evening reception/party was being held for fourteen policemen who had cycled to Amsterdam to raise money for Ronald McDonald House. I really wanted to go but Miranda played-up so badly that I could not take her. She kicked, head-butted and was quite violent towards me. Zöe went to see the policemen with Rudi and she was thrilled because she had her photo taken with all of them and they all made a fuss of her.

We occasionally visited Surrey Quay Shopping Centre. It was a modern, indoor shopping centre with a variety of shops. There were beautiful water fountains on the ground floor and escalators leading up to Burger King. I ordered lunch while Rudi minded the girls. When I came back with the burgers and chips Miranda was nowhere to be seen. Rudi had presumed that she was with me and I had presumed that she was with him. We panicked for a moment and then heard her screaming loudly in the distance. Rudi raced down the escalator towards Miranda's distinctive screams. She was getting into the shopping centre water fountains and was hitting the poor security guard who had tried to stop her by picking her up. Rudi was very embarrassed and so was the security guard who thought that Rudi was going to tell him off. We were relieved that Miranda was safe but worried at how quickly she could disappear and get into trouble.

Zöe and Miranda were usually very well behaved in the radiotherapy department. Our visits there had become a daily routine. Miranda was fascinated by the flashing red lights saying "Do not enter." She became very excited and bounced up and down gleefully whenever the lights appeared. It amused all the people waiting. She would make herself at home there and would lie in the middle of the waiting room floor reading "Spot the dog" books. I would often sit and read Zöe stories while we waited for treatment, well aware that most of the adults were listening to see how the stories would end.

There was a little radio in the waiting-room toy box. When you wound the handle, it would play, "Whenever you're afraid – whistle a happy tune." The girls played it over and over again. One day there was a new little girl waiting to have radiotherapy treatment and Miranda went up to her and gave her the radio. It was extremely unusual for Miranda to give another child a toy. The little girl's mother told us that her daughter had undergone nine operations since last August and was due to have another one. She was another very brave little girl.

Many of the adults remarked on how good the children were. One lady was very distressed when she found out that Zöe had a brain tumour. She had thought that I was the one waiting for treatment because my hair was short and spikey. Radiotherapy often caused hair loss and many patients had their hair cut very short.

Miranda liked the buttons in the hospital lifts which lit-up when you pressed them. If we did not stop her, she would press them all to see as many lights as possible. The drinks machines also appealed to her - she would often put an empty paper cup on her head and pretend it was a hat. She loved hats of all shapes and sizes. When a well-meaning visitor gave her a Cornetto ice-cream to eat she put that on her head too and I had to wash her hair.

Zöe longed to go to school again and see all her friends and teachers. Her friend at the hospital had gone home as his radiotherapy had finished and we promised to keep in touch with his family. Zöe wanted to go home too but she had a few more weeks of treatment left. I phoned her teacher quite regularly to tell her how Zöe was doing in London and asked her if Zöe could visit the school when we came home the following weekend. We stopped at a petrol station to buy some flowers for her teacher and some sweets for the children in her class. Then we took Zöe to school. Her headmistress came outside to meet us and took her to the classroom. Zöe was delighted to be at school again even if it was just for the Friday afternoon.

When we met Zöe at 3 o'clock her teacher told us that she had spent some time with her friends in her usual class and also some time with her other friends in her former class. Her teachers were worried because crowds of children had surrounded Zöe and welcomed her back but Zöe had coped well with the crowds and enjoyed all the attention. In fact Zöe seemed so well and so normal, sometimes it was hard to believe what was happening. Her hair loss was mostly at the back of her head but it did not seem to bother Zöe at all. She pulled out a chunk of her hair and put it on the back of Rudi's trousers. Then laughed and said, "Look daddy has a tail".

Throughout Saturday we had lots of visitors as usual and I took Zöe to a swimming pool birthday party which was great fun. Rudi went to church alone the next day so that the girls could rest. People were still fasting and praying for Zöe. We all hoped that her tumour would go and also that she would suffer no bad side effects from the radiotherapy. At home I tidied up as much as possible while Miranda relaxed and Zöe played. Then it was back to London again. Zöe sulked and was grumpy in the car. She did not like leaving all her friends behind.

I heard there was a really good swimming pool at the Elephant and Castle and took the children there. The water was quite shallow, the pool was well-supervised and it also seemed quite empty. There were frog and elephant-shaped slides. It was another place for us to go besides the swing parks, shops and riverside walks. After taking the children there several times I mentioned the pool to a nurse in the radiotherapy department. She told me that Zöe was not meant to go swimming as the chemicals in the water would irritate her skin because of the radiation.

More visitors came armed with presents and food for us and Zöe was pleased to see them all. Toys and presents were okay but not as good as real people to play with. We took our visitors to the HMS Belfast and along the river to the Hays Gallery. We also took them to our favourite park with the blossom trees and swings. We took my aunt and uncle for a riverside walk and my uncle bought us all an ice-cream. He paid three times the normal price for the ice-creams because he bought them from a place for tourists. Zöe tripped over Miranda and dropped her ice-cream. She cried and so he bought her another one. Then my aunt tripped and dropped her ice-cream so he bought her another one too. It was an expensive day out for them. Another of my aunts made Miranda a green jelly as she knew it was one of the only foods she would eat. She carried it on the train all the way to London.

Rudi's boss came to see us at Ronald McDonald House. British Telecom had organised a quiz night, in a room above a pub, at High Holborn, to raise money for Zöe. We all went along and they raised £250. Miranda would not sit still for long so I took her for an hour-long pushchair ride around Holborn and Covent Garden, which she enjoyed. I knew the area well from when I had worked in London. Zöe, meanwhile, had a great evening with Rudi and all his colleagues made a fuss of her. People were good to us. We still received lots of letters and cards from well-wishers. It was at times like this when we realised how many friends we had and how lucky we were.

Every day I would take Miranda and Zöe to the post office. We would send off all the letters and postcards we had written to our friends, but before we did anything else we had to buy Miranda a "Spot the Dog" birthday card. Once she had the birthday card to hold she would be good and we could go elsewhere. If we did not buy her a "Spot the Dog" card she would cry for ages and ages. There were two designs Miranda liked. One had "birthday girl" on the front and the other had "age 1". Once we returned to Ronald McDonald House, Miranda would forget about the card and I would put it with the others and keep it for someone's birthday. Most of our friends received "Spot the Dog" cards that year regardless of their age and we told them Miranda had chosen the card.

Miranda did not like pandas. There had been one at her playgroup that had frightened her and one on a "Spider" video we had seen. Now unfortunately Miranda had seen a panda in the ground floor playroom at Ronald McDonald House. Zöe had chased her around with it and Miranda was reluctant to go downstairs in case the panda was nearby. I spent ages amusing her in the bedroom by making dolls hats out of socks until I could persuade her to go downstairs.

Rudi became very ill with a tummy bug. We were all back in Whitstable for the weekend and he stayed in bed and slept nearly all day. It was lovely weather and Miranda and I sat on the front step whilst Zöe played with friends in the street. Zöe had a powerful water gun and was shooting everyone with it. Miranda had developed a liking for dogs and kept running after them, with me right behind her. The following day Rudi was still very ill and could not travel back to London with us. Zöe went to the seaside with some of our neighbours and then I took the children to my parent's house for dinner. In the afternoon, Pauline came and took the children and me up to London. We dropped my mother off at my aunt's house on the way so she could have an afternoon out. It was strange to go to Ronald McDonald House without Rudi.

My mother came up to London two days later with two aunts and another cousin's daughter. Miranda loved the little girl and ran around with her quite happily. My mother was pleased to see Ronald McDonald House. We all walked to Tower Bridge and alongside the River Thames and Zöe asked if her granny could stay with us until Rudi was better.

It was just as well she did because in the morning I was very sick and had a bad migraine. I took Zöe and Miranda to radiotherapy as usual and then when I came back I rested with Miranda whilst my mother took Zöe to buy me some migraine tablets. Zöe showed her around the Hays Galleria and took her for a walk to the HMS Belfast. My mum was impressed with the number of people who seemed to know Zöe and talked to her. Zöe asked the guide on the HMS Belfast how much it had cost to build the ship. He did not know and gave her a chocolate medal because he could not answer her question. She bought herself an HMS Belfast hat and lots of postcards for all her friends.

On Thursday morning my mother caught the train back to Whitstable. Miranda was very ill with a bad stomach upset and I was told to take her to the doctor in Casualty. There seemed to be some worry as to whether we had all caught a virus from someone in the hospital. I was expecting a really bad time as usually Miranda would kick, hit and refuse to take off clothes if she needed a medical examination. However she was really good and let the doctor examine her quite thoroughly. I was so surprised at how good Miranda was that I kept giggling. Zöe played with a giant toy donkey in the waiting room. She enjoyed visiting all the different hospital areas and seeing the variety of toys. I bought Miranda two "Spot the Dog" birthday cards that day as a reward for being so good.

In the afternoon I had volunteered to go along with one of Zöe's doctors to see a crowd of medical students. The girls were being cared for in the playroom nearby. The students all sat around in a circle and asked me questions about Zöe. They had to try and guess what was wrong with her. I gave them too many clues and they soon worked it out. After Zöe, they had to try and guess what was wrong with Miranda. They found this much more difficult. I really enjoyed the session and talking to the young students.

Miranda had dreadful tantrums on Thursday evening and Friday morning although she seemed quite well again. She had developed a dislike of being in the Ronald McDonald House kitchen area. This was a problem as we had a lot of our meals there. She also made sure that all the doors she passed in Ronald McDonald House were closed. She would go along the corridor closing them all. Her obsessions and dislikes just seemed to suddenly come from nowhere and for no apparent reason. I was pleased when Rudi turned-up on Friday afternoon. He had recovered from his virus. We stayed in London for the May Bank Holiday weekend and visited the Zoo, various parks and Blackheath funfair.

On the Wednesday I had a phone call from Casualty about Miranda's test results. I was told that Miranda had a urine and kidney infection. The doctors wanted her to see someone at Canterbury Hospital. I panicked as there were lots of children at Ronald McDonald House awaiting kidney transplants. I immediately worried that something might be seriously wrong with Miranda's kidneys. I felt guilty for being so angry with her earlier in the week when she had kicked me and screamed. I kept thinking of a lady in Whitstable who had said to me: "It's not fair that Zöe might die, she's such a lovely child. It should have been Miranda not Zöe." I had been shocked by this lady's remark. I suddenly felt really scared in case I was going to lose both my children. Fortunately, later when Miranda had her scan it showed that her kidneys were fine.

Zöe's ears were sore. We had stopped going swimming but I was sure the water had not caused this problem. The recent radiotherapy treatments had made her skin very itchy and now it was splitting. She had to have her ears painted with a purple liquid after the radiotherapy sessions. Zöe did not mind having this done at all. We had to wait for ages in the waiting room to see the radiotherapy doctor. Miranda was bored and screamed.

People gave her dirty looks but no-one said anything. At one stage whilst I was busy with Zöe, I saw Miranda climb onto a man's lap so she could reach the fish tank in the corner. The man was very disapproving. I dashed over and removed her before she caught a fish. A nurse who saw us, realised that Miranda liked water and took Miranda to play with water in the sink nearby so I could be with Zöe whilst she had her ears painted.

I ran out of nappies for Miranda and when Rudi came home from work I took her to Boots near London Bridge to buy some more. Zöe was tired and stayed with Rudi. I had to carry Miranda's pushchair up quite a few steps and a man offered to help me. Miranda did not like the idea of a strange man carrying her pushchair and tried to get out halfway up. However, when we reached the top of the steps she decided she did not want the man to go and would not let go of his hand. This was half amusing and half embarrassing. I had to queue for ages in Boots. Miranda hated waiting for anything and soon she was moaning and kicking me. My legs and ankles were bruised and aching from her constant attacks.

I took her back to Ronald McDonald house via McDonalds where she ate her daily chips. Whilst I was paying she ran off and walked around the various tables. I wanted to race after her but was in the middle of being served. Then to my horror I saw her try to take a man's drink and when he said "no" she kicked him. I apologised to him and explained that she was autistic and he was very nice about it. I vowed to take reins with me next time though it was difficult to hold Miranda on reins in one hand whilst balancing a tray full of food and drink in the other.
When Miranda and I returned from our walk we were delighted to see Zöe's best friend from Whitstable and her family. Zöe was very excited and I was really pleased to see her smiling. Not long ago her face had been so puffy that she seemed to have lost her smile. Now her facial muscles seemed to be working again. Zöe showed her friend all around the house, the playrooms and garden.

We had another weekend back in Whitstable during which Zöe fell and hit her head badly again. She slept for four hours and we were worried. It was boiling hot weather and the journey back to London was bad with heavy traffic. People were travelling back to London after a day out by the seaside. Miranda took off her seat belt when we were in the fast lane of the motorway and we had to pull over in a lay-by and put it back on her. We were pleased that this would be our last trip to London for a while.

Monday 7th June was to be our last day at Ronald McDonald House. Zöe bought lots of special medallions for her friends as a souvenir of her stay in London. She made a card for the nurses in radiotherapy with a clown on the front and gave them chocolates. She drew a picture of Noah's Ark and wrote a poem for the nurses in Guy's Hospital children's ward. She had come to know a lot of them very well. Miranda and I delivered lots of toys to various hospital wards after first going to buy Miranda a "Spot the Dog" card as usual. The girls had been given a lot of new toys and we had cleared-out quite a few of their other ones. We said goodbye to the cheerful hospital ward play-leader and to the doctors. It was sad to leave the lovely staff at Ronald McDonald House and sad to leave the friends we had made especially the other children who were still having treatment. The hospital doctor checked Zöe over and then we went home. We were told that we could phone the hospital anytime for advice and not to worry too much if Zöe fell or banged her head.

Zöe had completed her radiotherapy treatments with very few side-effects - hardly any headaches and no sickness. We wondered if it was because of all the prayers being said for her by friends, neighbours and people at our church. We hoped that her brain tumour had become smaller but would have to wait a few more weeks to find out.

It was a peaceful journey back to our house with our usual children's music tape playing in the car. Whitstable and the Kent countryside seemed more beautiful than ever, though Ronald McDonald House and the little Bermondsey park nearby would always have a place in our hearts.

Zöe wasted no time in going back to school - she loved it there. Whilst in London, Rudi and I had read her stories and we had done pieces of school-work as Zöe was eager to learn and to keep-up with her friends. She went to school with her best friend and wore a pretty pink dress with flowers. She looked beautiful and I felt very proud of her. The school had instructions to phone us at any time if they were worried about her but Zöe had a wonderful day and all seemed well.

Miranda woke-up screaming and hitting that night. She was due back at her playgroup the following day. I gave her a spoonful of medicine to make her sleep and then worried that she would not wake-up in time for the minibus in the morning. However, Miranda was fine the next day and enjoyed going back to playgroup.

We had the paddling pool out in the garden and lots of friends came to play after school again. Things seemed almost back to normal. Zöe had some new face paints and all the children in the road painted each other's faces and pretended to be butterflies or turtles. They also played with water guns and water bombs. It was glorious hot, sunny weather and they made the most of it. Zöe joined The Girls Brigade and was quite proud to go there. She went with two of her best friends. She was especially pleased when we bought her a Girls Brigade uniform. We were all determined to carry on as usual.

Miranda made friends with a large dog who lived in our road. She loved to watch him play and was especially fascinated by the fact that he drank out of a bowl on the floor. After seeing him, Miranda came home and poured her orange drink into a bowl. She put it on the floor and copied him. Fortunately she only did this once and it did not become a habit.

We went to church on Sundays as usual and often visited friends in Ramsgate whose children were about the same ages as Zöe and Miranda. They lived near to a park and the beach. Zöe's friend let her ride a small bicycle with no stabilisers, which she had outgrown. We were amazed at how good her balance seemed. We hoped this was a sign that the tumour had grown smaller.

Our doctor and the people at Miranda's playgroup were all eager to arrange for me to have extra help at home whilst Rudi was at work especially as the long summer holidays were coming. I asked at Miranda's playgroup if I could send Miranda to a local play-scheme for part of the August holidays. I wanted more time with just Zöe. I was reluctant to have people interfere with the normal running of my household. I wanted the children to be able to play and do the things they enjoyed. However, I could see that everyone wanted to help and agreed to have a social worker visit. She sent along a family support worker whose job was to play with Miranda and make friends with her. If I had to rush off somewhere suddenly with Zöe and no-one was available to mind Miranda, she would help out. I had family, friends and neighbours all around me so I could not see this happening but the lady who came was very nice and we all got on very well. Miranda liked her instantly, particularly because she wore a gold coat and big dangly earrings. Miranda was very interested in clothing and jewellery. I breathed a sigh of relief. She came once a week and we all enjoyed her visits.

By July, Zöe's face seemed puffy again and she was definitely becoming more tired. I hoped that I was imagining it but I was worried. We received a bill from the Maudsley Hospital for sending Zöe's scans to New York. We were expecting to hear very soon whether anyone in America could help her. All we could do was hope and trust in God.

Chapter 7 – Disneyland Paris and Afterwards

July 1993 – November 1993

We were offered a free holiday at Disney World in America, for all the family but we felt unable to travel that far with Miranda so we asked if we could go to Disneyland, Paris instead.

I gave Miranda a spoonful of medicine, prescribed by the doctor, to keep her calm on the journey and it seemed to work. Zöe loved being high above the clouds in an aeroplane and she wondered if you could sit on clouds or if you would fall through them. Our favourite video characters, "The Care Bears," lived in the clouds. When the aeroplane landed Zöe went into the Captain's cockpit and looked at all the dials etc. She was impressed.

We went by car to a Davy Crockett lodge in the woods at Disneyland, Paris. It was near to a miniature farm and both the children loved seeing all the animals. A Disney representative gave us a special pass for Zöe so that she could go to the front of any queue and would not have to line-up to go on any rides. A bus took us to the main Disneyland complex which was far more wonderful than we had expected. We loved the colourfulness of everything: the shows, the rides, the little old-fashioned shops and beautiful pink fairy-tale castle. We liked the popcorn and balloon sellers in their old fashioned costumes, the trams, police vans and characters. Everywhere we went we could hear music and see Disney characters. It was magical for us all. In the evening we went to see the electric parade with lights, carnival figures and fireworks. The children enjoyed all of it but Zöe was very tired and we had to keep resting.

By our third day at Disneyland, Paris, Miranda had decided that she would only go on a couple of rides. She was always making rules for herself about what she would and would not do. She particularly disliked the paddle steamer ride and screamed all the way along the river, which was a pity for everyone else on the trip. After that our family divided up and Zöe and Rudi went around all Zöe's favourite places. She enjoyed everything especially the Thunder Mountain ride. Miranda and I went on the "It's a Small World" ride all day over and over again. She was very happy!

Back at the Davy Crockett village both girls played near the farm and had a ride in a straw-filled cart pulled by a large horse. Miranda particularly liked the feel of the straw. Zöe talked to the lady who organised the horse and cart rides and the lady asked her why she had been in hospital. Zöe looked puzzled and said she could not remember. The magic of Disney had worked and made her illness seem far away. We finished the day by having a barbecue just outside our little log house.

Our journey home to England the next day was not a good experience. Zöe was upset because she was going home and kept crying. Miranda refused to put her seat belt on when the plane was landing and she fought with us and with the air-hostess.

It was horrible to be back. In Whitstable everyone was thinking about Zöe's brain tumour again. We went back to Guy's Hospital with Zöe on July 13th and waited over an hour to see the doctors. They did various neurological tests on Zöe. They tested her eyes, checked her knee and elbow reflexes, checked her shunt and hair growth, made her hop and do pigeon steps etc. They were quite friendly but we learned little from the examination. We were told again that we would hear soon from Dr Epstein in New York.

After our visit to the doctors we went to Rudi's office to see all our British Telecom friends and tell them about Disneyland. They had raised lots of money in case Zöe could have an operation in New York to remove the tumour.

At home, Zöe was happy and bouncy one day but tired and unwell the next. She had the occasional headache again and sometimes said her tummy was hurting. However, she was pleased to go back to school and to Girls Brigade again. She taught her grandparents Girls Brigade songs and dances. Zöe loved to sing songs to them and they taught her quite a few cockney and war-time ones. They played dominoes, draughts, cards, snakes and ladders and many other games with her. She had a special relationship with her grandparents and we felt very lucky that they lived so close.

On July 16th Zöe had a bad stomach-ache and seemed very tired. I kept her at home with me and called the doctor. A lady doctor came out and said she just thought Zöe had wax in her ears. I took Zöe out for a walk across the fields to the sweet shop where we always went. She complained that the light hurt her eyes and she seemed to walk higgledy-piggledy as if she was drunk. I hoped that was because her ears were blocked but I suspected the tumour was growing again.

Suddenly Zöe asked me, "Mummy, can you send a postcard from Heaven?"
I was alarmed.
"Why do you ask?" I said.
"Oh, I was just wondering….." Zöe replied.
"Well, if it is possible and I die first then I'll send you a postcard. If you die first then you can send me one. Hopefully neither of us would die for a long, long time."

Zöe seemed to accept this and we talked about other things. When we arrived home she seemed bright and breezy again. Later that day she went out to play on her bicycle with the children from two doors away and her balance seemed fine.

A new swing park had opened nearby and all the children were very excited about it. It was lovely to have somewhere so close to us for the children to go and play. A little boy at school asked Zöe if she had a hole in her brain and another child told her that she had a tumour in her eye. We had told Zöe that she had a brain tumour which caused her headaches and made her feel ill. She knew that the radiotherapy had been to try and get rid of it. We had not told her that she could die soon and we hoped that none of the other children would say anything. At church she was given lots of healing blessings for headaches, tiredness and her illness. Her health always seemed to improve straight afterwards but the symptoms would gradually return.

The August school holidays came and Miranda attended a special needs play-scheme at a school in Canterbury for a few days so that I could have some precious time alone with Zöe. Volunteers took the children on outings and played games with them back at the school. They always sent me home a note to say how she had behaved during the day and Miranda seemed to enjoy her days out. She went on an outing to Howletts zoo and let someone paint her face so she looked like a tiger. When she came home she was very proud and stood on the bed admiring her face in the bedroom mirror for most of the afternoon and evening.

I took Zöe out by pushchair, bus and taxi to wherever she wanted to go. We went to Herne Bay where she bought herself another pair of shoes. She had a particular love of shoes and had fourteen different pairs. Fortunately she had very cheap taste! We walked along the seafront and Zöe went on the trampoline, a bouncing castle, a roundabout, a helter-skelter and she drove a miniature car. It was lovely to spend time with just her and do all the things she wanted to do. We went to see Bambi at the cinema with some of Zöe's friends. They were excited about going on a bus as they went everywhere by car.

Zöe made friends with the little boy who lived across the road. They spent a lot of the week throwing toy boomerangs at each other. Zöe was annoyed as he could make his boomerang go back to him but she could not make her one work! She argued with him and he went home upset. Later his mother came over to see us. Zöe thought she was going to get told off for being grumpy and she hid under the bed upstairs. As it happened the little boy's mother had come over to give us a bag full of pretty dresses for the girls from her daughter. Zöe was delighted with them. She loved trying on clothes. Miranda was also very keen to dress-up and tried on eight dresses at once. She did not bother to take one off before putting the next one on.

Miranda liked to try on Zöe's clothes and play with her toys. When, Zöe was on the settee resting, Miranda would often cover her with a blanket or put a toy next to her. The girls loved each other very much. Occasionally Miranda would run around with Zöe and her friends. She would play chasing games or dance with them or join in pillow fights. It was good to see Miranda when she joined in with the others. Too often her play was repetitive and unimaginative and she often played by herself. The fact that she hardly spoke and she did not know what to do when other children spoke to her made things difficult.

The Education Department were creating a "Statement of Education" for Miranda. She had to see various officials who would submit reports saying why she needed to go to a "special education" school the following next year. I had written to a couple of the doctors who had failed to diagnose Zöe's brain tumour at the beginning of the year. I felt dubious about taking Miranda to see the same doctors. However, I felt better when I received an apology from one doctor who had not realised how ill Zöe was. He told me that he would bring her case up at a health meeting and see if he could get the reflex/co-ordination tests improved. He said he would also make other doctors more aware of brain tumour symptoms. He told me that he had not slept the night after receiving my letter because it was on his mind that he had failed to spot Zöe's symptoms. When Miranda and I saw this doctor he told me that Miranda had all round developmental problems as well as autism. She especially had very severe speech, communication and social skill problems. He did a good and thorough assessment of her which took over two hours. Miranda behaved well with him.

August arrived and we had days out at Herne Bay funfair, at the new swing park nearby and of course by the sea. Zöe went out quite a few times with her friend's families - they picked blackberries, had trips to the beach and looked for crabs and jellyfish! Miranda was playing more with the children who visited us every day and she was especially trying to join in Zöe's games. I thought how sad it would be if Zöe died just as Miranda was getting to know her and they were playing together. I wondered how it would affect the children who had played with Zöe since birth. I tried not to think about Zöe dying. After all, so many people were praying for Zöe that maybe she would live.

Simple things in life gave Zöe the most pleasure such as going to see her grandparents and playing in their garden. On one occasion, Zöe dressed up in a beautiful Hawaiian grass skirt and climbed my parent's apple tree. She was obviously feeling much better. Her strength seemed to come and go. Zöe asked her granny how she had caught "a brain tumour." She wondered if it was infectious like chicken-pox! Her granny assured her that it was not. She had just been unlucky.

My parents took Zöe and her best friend to Farming World for a day to see the animals there. They particularly liked the llamas and the muddy pigs. They took the children on a horse and cart ride around the orchard there. Zöe picked an apple from one of the trees and put it up her jumper. Her granny told the farmer how ill she was and he let her keep the apple.

Back at home Zöe and I perfected the art of making the biggest water-bombs to use during water fights when her friends came. We filled up about fifty water bombs by putting one end of a straw inside them and the other end up the tap – the children loved them. Some days about twelve children would play at the end of our cul-de-sac. They would ride their bikes, share each other's toys and generally have a good time. I was pleased that we lived in a road with so many children and pleased that I did not have to be at work but I could watch them all enjoying themselves.

Zöe and I often visited the Whitstable harbour and Lifeboat Station where her grandad helped in the souvenir shop. She loved to look at all the boats and even had a favourite one called "Sarah Jane". The Harbour had an open-day and Rudi climbed down a ladder with Zöe on his shoulders into a large boat so she could have a ride around the Harbour. Miranda and I watched them from the safety of dry land. When Zöe was too tired to walk Rudi would often carry her around on his shoulders and she much preferred this to being in a pushchair.

There was always a lot going on in Whitstable during August. The highlight of the month was the carnival. In the evening we all sat by the road to watch the carnival procession. We put pennies into buckets and collection boxes as the floats passed. The children held balloons, waved flags, blew hooters and ate lots of popcorn. It was a great evening out. I had always imagined that Zöe would be a carnival princess when she was older but now it seemed unlikely.

On 21st August we left sunny Whitstable for another holiday arranged by our British Telecom friends. This time we went to Butlins at Minehead. When we first arrived, we went on the monorail and Miranda threw her white polar bear and a blue pony from the top of the ride. They were gone by the time the ride ended and Miranda could not understand why we could not find them on the ground below. No doubt another child had taken them home to play with.

We loved the swimming pool with the fountains and special water features. Miranda would follow Zöe around as much as she could. We all enjoyed the evening entertainment and music at Butlins. Miranda would not sit down at a table for long and I would be walking around with her most of the time. Zöe particularly liked the Crazy Horse Saloon where we bought her a gun with some caps and an Indian Fancy Dress outfit.

In the daytime, we all went to the beach and Zöe had lots of donkey rides while Miranda and I paddled in the sea. We were lucky the weather continued to be so good. We bought more "Little Quint" dolls in the market for Miranda and a string-puppet for Zöe. At the end of the holidays Zöe bought lots of sticks of rock to take home for all her friends. She told me that she would like to stay at Butlins forever.

Holidays were great and a friend at British Telecom offered to pay for Zöe to go to Santa-land for Christmas. We did not tell her because we were not sure if she would be well enough to go. Christmas seemed a long way off.

Back at our house lots of children came to play as usual in the summer sunshine. A favourite game was mountaineering with Zöe's teddies. They tied all their skipping ropes together and hung them out of the bedroom window into the back garden. Zöe would tie a teddy to the end of the rope and they hoisted the teddy up the back wall of our house and through the window into the bedroom. As long as they used teddies and not children I did not mind.

Miranda had a friend who could be very assertive which was good for Miranda. She would insist that Miranda played with her and would not let Miranda run away. They both liked dressing up especially in funny hats.

September came and we were all very stressed. It was time to return to London and for Zöe to have another CT scan. We were told to arrive at Guy's Hospital before 9 a.m. so we had to leave really early to avoid the rush hour. Miranda was moaning and I felt angry with her even though her moans and tantrums were justified. We went for a walk along the Thames and looked at the HMS Belfast. Then we reported to the hospital day-care unit. They told us that Zöe would not need to be sedated for the CT scan after all and we should have come later they had made a mistake.

Both children wanted to go to the hospital playroom and play on the games console. I took them there for a while and all went well until a little boy came in with a drip and bag attached to him. Miranda walked over his wires and there was a pop. I thought, "Oh no, she's burst his bag," and I really panicked. However all was okay. She had only trodden on a balloon, which someone had left on the floor!

I removed Miranda from Guy's hospital before she caused any serious problems. I took the children to Ronald McDonald House for a while. Miranda was delighted to go back there and wanted to go in the lift where she pointed out G, 1 and 2 to me. Then she wanted to go to the turtle room where we had stayed but another family were using the room so we could not go inside. Miranda went to the playroom next and checked that the big black and white panda, which she disliked, was not there. Then she went in and played with the toys. I was delighted that she recognised some of the people there and she even said "Hello" to one of them.

At the day-care unit Zöe had to have some "magic cream" put on her hand and a needle with coloured dye inserted. She was very good although she hated wearing a bandage and the person who put the needle in bruised her hand badly. Miranda was fascinated by the numbers on Zöe's medical records and kept looking at them and saying "one, two." I was pleased that looking at numbers kept her quiet. Zöe was brave all through her CT scan and also afterwards whilst she waited for ages for someone to come and take off her bandage. We were told that the scan results would arrive in a week's time. Then we would know if the tumour had grown or disappeared. A week seemed ages to wait and we felt very frustrated.

On the last day of the summer holidays I stayed indoors so that Zöe's friends could come and play. Miranda screamed every time the front door opened and Zöe was aggressive and rude to me. Eventually she told me that she did not want to go back to school as she would miss being at home with me. I said that I would miss her as well and we both sat and cried.

In the morning Zöe left for school quite cheerfully. She was looking forward to seeing her friends and teachers again after all. Miranda and I went for a walk to the little shop across the fields. She bought a comic and a Kinder egg every time we went there. She also kept looking at the dog and cat food tins and wanted me to buy one. I realised that she thought a dog or cat was inside. Eventually I bought a tin, which we opened so she could see it contained only dog food. We gave it to a neighbour's dog.

During the school holidays Miranda had developed a numbers obsession and she looked for numbers everywhere. Back at home she was happy to study calendars, clocks and telephone directories for long lengths of time. I felt guilty that I did not have the energy to play with her as much as before. A friend brought me over an article about a new cancer drug and I spent all day phoning different places to try and find out more information about it.

After a few days at school Zöe was unwell again. She was tired and her eye looked as if it was turning inwards more. She complained of a headache and dribbled slightly – all bad signs. I kept her at home and we had a quiet weekend. Rudi and I could not concentrate on anything as we were so worried about Zöe's scan result. I spent a lot of the time making the children balloon animals and Rudi played lots of music. Zöe and her friends played as usual and seemed quite happy.

On Tuesday 14th September we left Miranda with my parents and drove to Guy's Hospital. We waited for over an hour in the outpatients with Zöe and as usual she was really good. The highlight of her day was when an enormous balloon which we had bought her, popped in the waiting room. It made a really loud bang and everybody jumped. She thought that was funny.

When we did eventually see the doctors the news was bad. Zöe's tumour was still there. They only had her recent scan and not any of the previous ones so they could not tell us whether the tumour was larger or smaller. We asked about various other new treatments and the doctors said they would look at the articles and suggestions I had given them and contact me but they were not hopeful. Zöe did not stay in the room with us while we all discussed her. She played with a helper outside. When the doctors had their break she went in to see them all and played with all the toys in their room. At home Zöe often played doctors and nurses with her friends. She was very good at remembering all the doctors' mannerisms and expressions.

Rudi and I were devastated at the news that the tumour was still there. Where was the miracle we had all prayed for?

A lady whose son had grown up with Zöe phoned to ask if Zöe could be a bridesmaid at her wedding in March. Zöe had always wanted to be a bridesmaid so we hoped it would be possible. She loved to dress-up in old lace curtains and play weddings with her friends. When a doctor from Guy's Hospital phoned me I mentioned the wedding but she said Zöe would much too ill by March to be a bridesmaid. It seemed that none of the treatments I had suggested to the doctor would be any good in the case of Zöe's brain tumour.

Rudi and I had a dreadful week but Zöe seemed in good spirits. She went to Girls Brigade as usual and the Girls Brigade Captain phoned to say that Zöe had said a lovely prayer and impressed everyone there. She had prayed for her friend who felt sick and a Girls Brigade leader with a bad ankle. People at most of our local churches were praying for Zöe. Many of them were convinced that she would be cured and we would see a miracle. Rudi and I still believed it was possible.

Luck did not seem to be on Zöe's side. Only hours after the hospital visit, she was playing with a little boy who climbed on top of a garden wall. He dislodged two bricks, which fell down missing Zöe's head by an inch. He ran away and left her shaking. Our neighbours saw the incident and said that Zöe was lucky not to have been killed! A few days later Zöe was very sick after eating some flowers from the honeysuckle bush in our garden.

Lots of Zöe's friends were having dancing lessons and we had been to watch them in a show during the summer. Zöe wanted lessons too and asked if she could go with them. The classes were very structured and the teacher seemed strict - I wondered if Zöe would cope. I let her go and she had a lovely time and thoroughly enjoyed dancing. She came home feeling very proud. She was living life to the full but I could tell she was very tired.

I had a phone call on 24th September from one of Zöe's doctors at Guy's Hospital. She told us that the tumour had not shrunk at all but just changed in shape. Things looked very serious. I asked again about a new drug called Temozolomide that was being used to treat tumours. The doctor said they were willing to use it on Zöe but were not happy about it because it was a chemotherapy drug and the side effects were bad. There was less than a one in a hundred chance of success. She asked if we really wanted to put Zöe through another lot of suffering when she would probably die anyway? She gave us until Tuesday to think about it. I phoned Cancer Research to find out more about it. The main side effects seemed to be hair loss, sickness and a weakened immune system.

I phoned Rudi at work to tell him the bad news about the tumour still being large and also about the chemotherapy drug. He was devastated and so were his colleagues. It seemed like the end of the road. We both spent the next couple of days trying to decide whether to give Zöe the treatment or not. We could think of nothing else. It felt strange having to do all our normal every day chores whilst our minds were just on Zöe. We went to Tesco as usual on Saturday to get the weekly shopping. Miranda was extremely good and walked around with us instead of sitting in the trolley. She spent ages admiring herself in the mirrors between the rows of shelves and looking at her reflection in the shiny metal ridges around the freezer shelves.

We went to a shop in Tankerton and bought Zöe a leotard, ballet shoes and leggings for her dancing lessons. She was thrilled and she came home, dressed up in her ballet clothes and showed Miranda all the ballet steps that she had learned. Miranda was impressed. She dressed up in Zöe's girls brigade clothes first and then in Zöe's leotard. She wanted to be like Zöe.

Rudi looked after Miranda in the evening. She was excellent with him and even said "Good night." She very rarely said that. She only used a handful of words regularly apart from numbers.

I went with Zöe to a celebration tea with the Girls Brigade at the local Baptist Church. We had a really good evening - Zöe and her friends danced and sang on the stage with the rest of the Girls Brigade then various other people entertained us. Many of the Baptist church leaders told me that they were praying for Zöe and would pray that we would make the right decision regarding the chemotherapy treatment.

At our own church the next day Rudi and I discussed what we should do with our church leader. He said he felt that Zöe should have the chemotherapy and that a miracle would happen and she would be cured! I mentioned the words of the blessing given to Zöe in Canterbury hospital. We had been told she would not be forgotten and angels would look after her. Our church leader said that he felt the blessing meant that Zöe would be looked after on earth by angels and would stay alive. I said I was sure it meant that she would be looked after by angels in Heaven. We all talked at some length. He told me that he felt Zöe had not yet been cured because of my lack of faith. I was not positive enough!

I left the church feeling angry that I was being blamed for no miracle because of my lack of faith when in fact I had so much faith. I felt angry that Zöe was going to have to go through chemotherapy. Why could God not have cured her before? Why should she have to suffer? I had no answers.

On Tuesday 28 September I phoned Guy's Hospital. It was exactly six months since Zöe's sixth birthday and it seemed the longest six months ever. Rudi and I both agreed to go ahead with the chemotherapy. There was no other choice except death. We both still believed that a miracle could happen. Zöe's doctor at Guy's told me that they were thinking of using a drug called "Etoposide" on Zöe because they could not get hold of any "Temorolozide" until November. The doctor seemed reluctant to tell me any details about the drug. I phoned Cancer Research, my local doctor and the Canterbury hospital doctor. Cancer Research were the most helpful in telling me the possible side effects – hair loss, sickness, low resistance to infections and white blood cells being killed. Zöe would need regular blood tests to check her blood count. It all sounded horrible. I was especially worried that Zöe would have to go back to Guy's Hospital and be put on a drip.

I took Zöe to her Girls Brigade Service in the evening. She was awarded two badges - one for physical and one for spiritual achievements and given a bookmark to commemorate the 100th anniversary of Girls Brigade. Zöe looked very smart in her uniform and we all felt very proud of her. She rushed up to the front to collect her badges and everyone told her to be careful as they could see her balance was not very good.

I kept Zöe at home the following day as she was very tired. She enjoyed school but I only wanted her to go when she felt well enough. Miranda was most annoyed that she had to go to The Mary Sheridan Centre when Zöe could stay at home. I took Zöe down to Whitstable and bought her a silver cup (from the Cancer Research shop) as a present for doing so well at Girls Brigade. We also bought a blue sequin belt and a glittery gold bag to use when she went dancing. I wanted Zöe to have precious, sparkly things and to feel special.

The next day Zöe went to school and Miranda stayed at home because there was no playgroup on a Thursday. Our friend, who had helped at the Mary Sheridan Centre came round and offered to take Miranda out in her car. Miranda was really happy to see her and shouted "Yes, yes, yes," when she arrived. It was very rare that Miranda enjoyed seeing someone. Miranda had a wonderful morning and our friend brought us back a tray of chocolate cakes she had baked. She told me that everyone at her church in Canterbury were praying for Zöe to get better and her own daughters prayed for her every day.

Miranda had developed some amazing skills with numbers. She showed me a new book with pictures of birds in trees. There were over fifty birds on one page and Miranda could tell me the exact number of birds just by looking at them - she did not seem to need to count them. I tried it with other pictures and she was remarkably fast at saying the number of objects on any page. At playgroup she would still go off alone and play by herself when she was allowed but at home she joined in simple games with Zöe and her friends.

Zöe went dancing after school and came back tired. She told me that dancing had been very hard work. She fell asleep at her friend's house and then on our settee when I brought her home. A little girl knocked and asked to play with Miranda. I was thrilled that another child wanted to play with Miranda rather than Zöe as children rarely asked to play with her. Unfortunately Miranda would not play and ran away. The little girl did not go home, instead she lied down on the settee and cuddled up to Zöe and pretended to be asleep.

October 1st came and Zöe was tired and sick again. We were meant to be returning to Guy's Hospital to discuss the chemotherapy idea. Instead I stayed at home with Zöe and Rudi went there alone. When Zöe felt a little better we visited a friend who lived around the corner and had two rabbits. Zöe loved the rabbits and I wondered how long we could last out before buying her a pet. My friend had a son who was Zöe's age and he lent her a small computer to play with. Her right hand seemed to be getting weaker but she could type well.

Rudi returned from Guy's Hospital with the chemotherapy drug called 'Etoposide.' We had to see our own doctor first to check that Zöe was well enough to start the treatment. Zöe was very good but she hated the idea of taking foul tasting medicine. We bribed her by saying she could have a Ferraro Rocher chocolate every time she had a spoonful. We found that Zöe preferred to take the medicine from a syringe squirted straight down her throat rather than on a spoon – that way she could not taste it.

After a rest Zöe seemed well and returned to school. I took Miranda for another assessment at the Mary Sheridan Centre. She saw a doctor that she particularly did not like. I could see the dislike in Miranda's eyes the moment she spotted her. She took one look at the doctor and said "Bye" and I knew that we were in for a hard time. The doctor was very firm with her and talked to her really harshly. She made Miranda sit on my lap and forced her to do activities like bathing dollies and putting pieces into puzzles. If Miranda refused to do something she would keep on asking her until she did it. Miranda was angry and she head-butted, hit and kicked me in her eagerness to try and get away from me and the stern doctor. When the doctor told her "no," Miranda hit her as well. This was the worst that Miranda had been for a long while. She did not like being forced to do things or being spoken to so harshly.

I was very embarrassed and smiled which the doctor took to be a sign that I approved of Miranda's behaviour. Things went from bad to worse and I was pleased when the assessment was over. I was told that Miranda's developmental age for understanding language was about age one and she had other developmental problems but she could do puzzles meant for a child of about age four.

I asked if Miranda could have a scan so that I could make sure she did not have a brain tumour like Zöe. The doctor agreed, probably just to put my mind at rest.

The following day Miranda went for a hearing test. We saw the same lady who had tested Miranda as a baby. She told me that she had thought something was wrong with Miranda apart from her hearing when we saw her all those years ago. She recognised us immediately and was very nice. Miranda was good and co-operative and the hearing test seemed fine. At playgroup they were still trying to potty-train Miranda. On one occasion the playgroup leader took her nappy off and put her into a pair of knickers. Miranda immediately took the knickers off and put them on the little boy who was standing next to her.

After only one week's chemotherapy Zöe was getting tired so I kept her off school. I went to my own doctor's surgery to try and find out when Zöe should have blood tests and when we should receive the next lot of chemotherapy medicine. He did not seem to know much about it and phoned Guy's Hospital who phoned me to say could Rudi pick up more medicine from them. It was lucky that Rudi worked nearby.

Zöe's blood test was to be the following Monday - I dreaded it and felt ill all weekend. Zöe was tired and we had lots of visitors again. They were good at keeping Miranda occupied but Zöe and I were not able to rest very much. At church people seemed more and more convinced that a miracle was going to happen and that Zöe would survive. I felt bad for having doubts in case my doubts were stopping the miracle. I tried to convince myself completely that she would get better and to make myself have more faith.

Unfortunately when it was time to go for Zöe's blood test, I had to take Miranda with me as well. Her playgroup bus had not arrived and no-one was around to mind her. Zöe was as good as gold at the doctors. She had to go in alone for her blood test because Miranda screamed so much that I was told to take her away. I felt really frustrated that again I was with Miranda when Zöe needed me more. Zöe seemed tired again and her speech was slurred. She was walking like a drunk and I was worried.

When Zöe's friends came to play I could see that Zöe had a lot less energy than before. She did not want to admit it and went to school, girls' brigade and dancing whenever she could. Two weeks after the chemotherapy had started we took Zöe and Miranda to a school disco and had a great night out with everyone enjoying themselves. The following day we went to an indoor adventure playground at Zöe's request. We felt proud of her because she wanted to do so much but it seemed as if her body could not keep up with her. She was spending more time at home with me between activities and just going to school when she felt well enough.

A friend offered to sell us a Sega games console with "Sonic the Hedgehog" games. This was wonderful because Zöe could play on the games console while she was resting. She liked it so much that Rudi bought her a Super Nintendo games console as well so she had even more to do at home. She liked to keep her mind active and all her friends like to come and play games as well. I bought Zöe a beautiful little green armchair especially made for children so that she could sit comfortably while she played the games. She was the envy of all her friends.

The school phoned me one day to say that Zöe was tired and could she come home at dinnertime. Then they phoned again to say that she refused to go home until after she had eaten her school dinner because it was spaghetti bolognaise. We all thought it was hilarious that she liked school dinners so much. Various people asked Zöe round to have spaghetti bolognaise dinners with them after that!

On October 25th I took Zöe and Miranda to a friend's house who lived next to some woods. We took her dog for a walk among the trees but Zöe was too weak to walk and I had to carry her back to the house.

The next day we went to Guy's hospital for a check-up. We waited three hours to see a doctor although we had made an appointment in advance. The doctor said she felt that the chemotherapy was not working and the tumour was growing. Zöe was tired and weak. Her speech was slurred, her balance was bad and there was a slight loss of feeling in her right arm and hand. The doctor recommended that we should stop the chemotherapy but Rudi and I begged for just one more try. We could not give up and let her die. Zöe loved life too much.

We had planned a Halloween Party as Zöe loved the idea of everyone dressing-up and playing games. She helped me to fill up all the party bags with little spiders and spooky toys. However, by October 29th she was clearly too weak to have a party and we cancelled it. Another neighbour held one instead so that all the children we had invited would not be disappointed. Zöe kept sleeping and was hardly eating. She was also suffering with diarrhoea and we worried about dehydration. She barely noticed the people who came to visit her because she was so tired.

She was taken into Canterbury Hospital and put in a little cubicle on her own. I stayed with her and slept on the edge of her bed. Every couple of hours I carried her to the toilet and back. She was too weak to walk. It was terrible to see a child who was usually lively and full of fun deteriorating so quickly. Zöe was very weepy and very cross because she was in hospital and missing the Halloween party. The doctors had discussed putting her on a drip because of dehydration but she started to drink a lot again and began to look better. Her blood count had gone far too low but now the chemotherapy had stopped, blood tests showed that it was rising again, which was good.

We were allowed home and Zöe was relieved to be out of hospital. People came from our church and we were told that eight hundred people had prayed for Zöe at a conference that weekend. Prayers were being said all over the world for her.

We took her back to Canterbury Hospital for a check-up and doctors told us that Zöe had lost most of the use in her right hand and arm. Her right leg also seemed limp but she could still walk. After her check-up we took her to Canterbury and she happily ate a meal in Burger King and bought some chocolate in Woolworths. When we arrived home all her friends came in to play and Zöe giggled in the corner with them.

Rudi took some time off of work to help me look after the two girls. Miranda caught tonsillitis and we struggled to try and give her medicine. She would close her mouth tightly and clench her teeth together. At times I had to wrap her in a towel so that her arms and legs were not free to hit and kick me. I would prise her teeth open carefully so she did not bite me and Rudi would give her a spoonful of the antibiotic.

When Miranda and Zöe both seemed a little better we took them to Canterbury shopping and bought them some toys for their Littlest Pet Shop collection. On the way back we visited the woods at Harbledown. The colours of the autumn trees were beautiful. Rudi carried Zöe through the woods so that she could see the beautiful leaves. He went passed two boys on their bikes and they looked alarmed.

So many people asked me if Zöe had suffered a stroke that I phoned the doctor and asked him. He said the limpness in her right side was caused by the brain tumour. Parts of her body were also very cold compared to the rest of her and the doctor said this was due to a problem with the blood vessels. I had never expected this gradual deterioration. I had always believed that Zöe would be well and maybe would just be tired and die in her sleep if the worst was to happen.

We had a wonderful fireworks evening in November. Over twelve of Zöe's friends came and Rudi put on a marvellous display in the garden. We all sung "For he's a jolly good fellow" at the end and shouted "Hip hip hooray." Afterwards two of our neighbours took Zöe to the school fireworks display with their children. When she was too tired to walk they gave her a piggy-back.

The following week seemed grey and dull after our lovely weekend. We were all tired and I had tonsillitis. I took Zöe for another blood test. More of her hair had fallen out and the rest seemed to be in terrible condition. She was very good about it but would only let me cut her hair if I pretended to be a horse. I gave her eleven rides up and down the room. I managed to cut away the matted hair and shape the rest into a bob leaving it much longer on one side. It looked good just like the unusual styles in top hairdressing salons. Zöe loved it.

We visited Canterbury Hospital again and saw our local specialist. He told me that Zöe's tumour was called a "Glioma." He drew me a picture of the brain and the brainstem cells and explained what was happening to her. Zöe meanwhile was playing with the toys outside in the play area. When the doctor asked her if she had any questions for him she said, "Yes, are you going to buy me a Christmas present?" I was pleased she was such a positive and optimistic child.

Chapter 8 – Hoping for a Miracle

November 1993 - March 1994

The chemotherapy was Zöe's last chance of survival. We were told that Zöe could start it again in mid-November as her blood count was high enough. We were worried as she was very tired and weak but we had to go ahead. We decided to put the Christmas tree up early to take Zöe's mind off the treatment and also just in case she did not survive until Christmas.

Zöe and her friends helped to decorate the tree and we put the Christmas lights on. Miranda was the most excited of everyone. She ran around the room in a Santa hat and gold beads laughing with joy. She wanted me to turn off all the main lights in the evening so that she could see the fairy lights glisten and sparkle.

Zöe was at home with me most of the time now and Rudi took time off work when he could. I pushed Zöe around in a pushchair as she was too ill to walk. She needed all her strength for when her friends came to play after school. Zöe talked about dying.

She said to her granny and me, "When I die I'm going to leave my money to Guy's Hospital and Ronald McDonald House." We assured her that we were all trying our best to make her better and she said, "It's not that bad to die – at least you get a rest."

We wondered if she was depressed because she could not go to school. There was a flu epidemic and fourteen of Zöe's classmates were ill so she had been advised to stay at home. Lots of the children who were well still came to see her but we had to be very careful that she did not catch any germs – her immune system might not cope.

We left Zöe at my parent's house on November 17th and took Miranda to Canterbury Hospital to have a CT scan. We wanted to make sure that she did not have a brain tumour like Zöe. She was good for the first hour at the hospital and then got bored waiting to be weighed. I took her shoes off so she could not kick anyone as I could sense she was getting agitated. I dragged her off to the playroom but unfortunately it was being used for school lessons so we could not play in there. We wandered around the hospital and then went to the waiting room again. There was another hour's wait and Miranda screamed all the time. She hated waiting.

When it was eventually her turn to have the scan, I sat her on my lap while the anaesthetist blew gas into her mouth and then she went straight to sleep. While she slept one of the staff offered to give her a manicure. Her finger and toe nails were cut neatly and filed when we went to collect her afterwards. I thought this was quite amusing and a very good service. We collected Miranda after an hour and she was soon wide-awake and very angry. She refused to go into the bed on the children's ward and sat in her pushchair. The hospital staff wanted her to rest a while after the anaesthetic but Miranda put on her coat and made it very clear that she wanted to go home. After much discussion she was allowed to go home with us. This was a relief for all the other sick children trying to rest on the ward. As soon as we got home Miranda cuddled me and kept kissing me. She was so grateful to not be in hospital. She was also wide-awake but Rudi and I were exhausted.

Zöe came home and told us she had had a good time at her grandparents.

As Zöe went to sleep she said to me "Goodbye – I'll be gone in the morning. I'm going to kill myself so I don't have to take any more medicine."

Rudi and I were really worried. We had a long talk with Zöe about all the reasons she needed to take the medicine and get better. After reminding her of possible holidays, toys, funfairs and things she could do if she got better she brightened up a little and said maybe she would take the medicine.

Zöe's friends continued to come and cheer her up regularly. It snowed and we were all very excited. I pulled the children along on sledges but Zöe had problems holding on because her right hand was so weak. She felt frustrated that she could not run around with the other children. One of her friends built a snowman in the back garden with her. We were careful to dress Zöe in very warm clothes so she did not catch a cold. She seemed happier outside. Miranda also loved the snow and kept putting on different hats and scarves.

Zöe and Miranda seemed to be fighting a lot, sometimes over toys but at other times they just both seemed frustrated – Zöe with her illness and Miranda because she did not understand what was happening. I often had to put Miranda in the bath to calm her down - she loved baths with lots of bubbles. Strangely enough the bubbles did not seem to affect her eczema.

During those winter weeks, I took the children out by taxi to various places. It was too stressful to be indoors all the time. Neighbours, family and friends also all offered to take Zöe out. On one occasion we went with my sister Olive and little Joel to an indoor adventure playground at Margate. Both girls loved the adventure playground especially the slide and ball-pool. Zöe's limp was much worse and her balance was not very good. Her hair was falling out in big clumps and one of her eyes was turning inwards again. Sometimes her hand would not work properly. I noticed people staring at her and one lady asked me if she could speak and understand things! I was very upset by this question – they did not realise how bright and clever she was. Zöe had a brilliant mind.

While I was helping Zöe, Miranda was up to all kinds of mischief. She took her nappy and trousers off at the adventure playground and ran around without them until I caught her and put them back on. Then she saw two little girls hitting each other and she went up to them and hit them both. She did not like people fighting! She led a lady to the souvenir counter and tried to make the lady buy her a toy. The lady did not understand what Miranda was saying and thought she was lost. When I explained that she was autistic the lady looked embarrassed and uncomfortable.

I was pleased when December arrived and there was so much more to do with Christmas on the way. I took Zöe out in the pushchair to see Father Christmas at Canterbury and we looked at the decorations in the shops. It was getting more and more difficult for Zöe to walk and she tripped if she tried to walk too far. When we came home I phoned the Social Services and asked if I could get a walking frame for Zöe. Her right hand was not strong enough to grip a walking stick and her balance was deteriorating. I also noticed she was dribbling more and her speech was less distinct.

Zöe longed to be at school so I phoned the school and asked if she could go in for just a few hours. She was so eager and not worried about looking different or about her bald patch. She refused any offers of hats or wigs. I really admired her for not caring about her appearance. At school lots of the children, teachers and classroom helpers were ready to help Zöe in any way that they could. She wanted me to go home and leave her alone so she could be independent.

Her teacher phoned later and said Zöe wanted to stay all day long. She had been giggling and quite happy throughout the day. However, she had been unable to eat much of her school dinner because it was difficult for her to hold any cutlery. She also was unable to do cutting, drawing or play on the computers. Her right hand had become stiff like a claw and her right leg often seemed to stick in a tiptoe position. The school said they would provide a special helper to be with her when she was able to attend.

Zöe came home quite cheerful but very tired. She watched her friends leave for Girls Brigade without her whilst she sat and rested. She never complained and would not admit it if she was upset. However, she asked me if when people died they were given new taller bodies and new brains.

Zöe's best friend came to sleep for the night at our house. Both of them giggled, messed around and pushed Miranda out of the bed when she wanted to sleep with them.

Zöe asked to go to the Indoor Adventure Playground again. We tried to put her off going there, thinking that she would not be able to cope with it. Rudi told her she could only go there if she managed to walk up and down the room three times. She did it easily - her determination was remarkable.

The Lions Christmas float passed by outside and I remembered when Rudi had dressed up as Father Christmas at the church Christmas party. Zöe had been his Christmas fairy and had helped to give out the presents. It was hard to watch the float go past and hear all the carols knowing that Zöe was so ill.

The blood test at the doctor's the next day showed that her blood count was fine. However, we doubted that the chemotherapy was working. Zöe's speech was becoming so slurred that we found it hard to understand her sometimes and naturally that made her feel very frustrated. People kept asking if we were going to celebrate Christmas early.

Zöe's friends came as usual and told me they were going to make silver cups from aluminium foil and play racing games with Zöe. This worried me a bit but then I noticed that the children helped Zöe make a cup and they let her win some of the races - she did not seem to mind.

Zöe seemed quite cheerful but she was asking more questions about Heaven which of course we could not answer. We were trying to stay positive and to believe that Zöe would still get better. The prayers and healing blessings continued but a miracle seemed more and more unlikely. It was now out of the question that we would take Zöe to see Father Christmas in Sweden, as planned, or go anywhere for the Christmas holidays. She was not well enough. We had also heard from America that her tumour could not be operated on. British Telecom told us to use the money they had raised to buy lots of presents and give the girls a good Christmas.

Rudi and I went to Zöe's school to watch her in the Christmas play. Every class put on a play about kings and queens. Zöe was the duchess in her play and wore a silver hat with a pink ribbon. She sat next to her helper and stayed close to her as she shuffled along. After school she went up to her schoolteachers and gave them big hugs. She was very fond of the teachers and helpers and they all took good care of her. I could see that all the other parents were very upset when they saw Zöe in the school play and we were upset as well.

On December 14th we left Miranda at a friend's house and took Zöe back to Guy's Hospital. We saw Zöe's doctors and they said that the chemotherapy had not worked. Zöe would probably die around Easter-time. There was nothing else they could do. It was the news we had been dreading. The doctors said we could go to the Royal Marsden hospital for a second opinion and we said we would.

I took Zöe with Miranda to the Mary Sheridan Centre Christmas party the following day. It seemed strange to go to hospital one day and then to a party the next, but that was life. We had to take one day at a time and make the most of every opportunity for Zöe to have a good time. At the party there was a man who made model animals out of balloons. Zöe was eager to stand up at the front and help him. I had to stand behind her because she was unsteady on her feet and everyone thought she might fall.

The physiotherapist showed us some electrical toys that would help Zöe get around – an electric car and an electric dalek with a seat inside. They were not National Health Service items but gifts that had been donated to the centre. Zöe was excited about them and Rudi brought them home in his car. Her friends came to play and they all zoomed around.

One little girl said to Zöe, "I wish I could be ill like you so I could have an electric car."

Zöe went to school for Christmas dinner – she had not wanted to miss it. The school holidays were coming and I wondered if this would be the last time she would be able to go to school.

The following day we went to The Royal Marsden Hospital. Zöe and Miranda played happily in the play area while we talked to the doctor. He had looked at the scans and agreed that nothing more could be done for Zöe. Her tumour was an aggressive one resistant to both radiotherapy and chemotherapy. It was dreadful coming home in the car. We were all very upset and Zöe tried to talk to us but her speech was so slurred that we could not understand what she was saying. She became frustrated and upset Miranda and we all wanted to cry.

When Zöe's friends came in to play it lightened the atmosphere and cheered her up. I kept thinking how Zöe's friends were like little rays of sunshine in the gloom. We were so grateful that they kept coming to play through the bad times as well as the good ones.

We missed church. It was more and more difficult to go there. We knew if we went, we would face a barrage of questions about how Zöe was doing. Talk of miracles did not help and we just did not feel like facing the well-wishers. On Sunday afternoon, some friends from church called in to see us. They were cheerful and their children played well with Zöe. They were also realistic about Zöe being ill and could see that it was unlikely she would be cured. They told us there were mixed feelings at our church. Many people still expected Zöe to be healed and a miracle to happen but others were now doubtful. A few people said they would leave the church if a miracle did not happen.

The Royal Marsden Hospital had given us steroids to use for Zöe. They made her feel really good but slightly puffy and bloated. They also increased her appetite and she ate ten ice-creams one day. She was developing a slight cough and seemed to be finding it difficult to swallow solid foods so ice-cream seemed the perfect food. We went to Canterbury Hospital and saw the doctor there. Zöe was too ill to stand-up and be weighed so she had to sit on chair-scales instead. She also had to lie down to be measured. The doctor gave us laxative medicine for her and told us to reduce the steroids slightly.

Meanwhile at the Mary Sheridan Centre I had been told that Miranda would probably have trouble getting into our local autism unit which was on the premises of the Zöe's school. It was full-up and there were no spaces there. I was furious as Miranda would be five years old in April and since she was just two years old different officials had always led us to believe that she would get a place there. There were no other schools for autism locally at all. There was a mixed disability school in Canterbury but we were not even sure that she could have a place there.

This seemed a cruel blow. How were we meant to cope with two children at home: one dying and seriously disabled and the other with autism and needing lots of attention? We felt very angry and I contacted the various doctors we knew and all the officials I could think of, to ask them to write letters to help Miranda get a place at our local autism unit. On Wednesday 22nd December, our local M.P. came to see us. He stayed for a while and met the children. Then he wrote a letter to the local education office on our behalf. We were very grateful for his time and his help. We hoped it would make a difference.

We took the children to Toys'R'Us and bought them everything they wanted for Christmas. We also had Sky TV installed so that there would be more programmes on television for the children to watch. We realised that it was becoming more and more difficult for Zöe to play with toys as her body was becoming weaker. Miranda's favourite presents were the characters from a Jungle Fun Train and lots of little Mr Blobbys which fitted onto the tops of pencils. Zöe's favourite presents were a Little Tikes Cottage and a pair of pink self-tying shoe-laces which were a marvellous invention for children unable to tie up their shoes. I thought of the time when Zöe removed Rudi's brown shoe-laces from his best shoes and threaded-in pink ones instead.

Miranda was unhappy when she woke-up on Christmas morning and so I had to take her out. I pushed her in the pushchair down to the sea and when someone stopped me to ask how we were I could not stop crying. The only thing that would make my Christmas happy was for Zöe to get better and it did not look like this was going to happen. However, back at home we all stayed as cheerful as we could manage. Rudi cooked the Christmas dinner. Zöe seemed quite jolly and her speech seemed much clearer, her eyes seemed straighter and she seemed to have regained some movement in her right hand.

Both girls went back to school on January 5th. Miranda went back to the Mary Sheridan Centre and was happy once she settled there. Zöe was excited to see all her friends and had a lovely day. When I took her to the school two little girls rushed up and gave her a hug, then gave me a hug as well.

I had a phone-call from The Mary Sheridan Centre playgroup to say that Miranda was allowed to go there full-time because of the situation with Zöe. It was strange to have a week with no children at home in the daytime and I missed them. Rudi had three months leave from work so he could be with Zöe. He took her to school when she was well enough to go there and he ran Miranda to playgroup and back.

When Zöe was at home she rested on the settee and slept a lot. In between Zöe would do drawing and watch television. She did lots of drawing with her left hand and managed to take the pen caps on and off with her toes because her right hand would not work. She made a little book with lots of drawings about one of her favourite videos "Button Moon."

I took her to see Snow White and The Seven Dwarfs at the Marlowe Theatre in Canterbury. We went to Debenhams first where there was a cave filled with beautifully polished coloured stones. We spent ages choosing the prettiest stones which Zöe put into a little treasure chest. Occasionally she shared her treasure with friends and people who were good to her. We took Zöe swimming too as she loved the water. Her teachers had bought her a special swimming costume with floats all the way round, so she could move about safely.

Miranda meanwhile was spending a lot of time with a friend and her two daughters when she was not at playgroup. She seemed very happy and enjoyed being taken to their house. She loved their big friendly dog and their yellow canary.

I felt that we were pushing Miranda away from us but we had to give Zöe priority. The atmosphere at our house upset Miranda. She did not like a lot of the programmes that Zöe watched. She would stand in the hallway and peer through the cracks in the door at the television but sometimes would be afraid to come inside because of a certain advert or television character. She also could not understand that Zöe was ill and sometimes needed peace and quiet so she could sleep. Miranda liked to run around noisily and it was difficult for her to be quiet for more than a few minutes. Most of all she disliked the constant stream of visitors coming to see us. It was too much for her to cope with.

A friend who we had known years ago came to see us. He believed in the power of healing and blessed Zöe that she would recover and lead a normal life. In his blessing he said that although medical cures had not worked the power of God would heal her. I was worried about this blessing but another friend from our own church still insisted that God would heal Zöe and he was excited that someone else had confirmed it would happen. She would be healed on this earth the blessing had said – she would not have to die first and go to Heaven before she was healed.

After the blessings we decided to involve as many people as possible in our efforts to persuade God to heal her quickly. We chose a special day, February 6th and wrote a letter to over thirty churches in our area telling them about Zöe's illness. We asked them to pray and fast for a miracle to happen on that day. We also contacted friends around the world who in turn contacted their local churches so that thousands of people everywhere would be praying and fasting for Zöe on February 6th. We put a notice in the Daily Telegraph newspaper asking all their readers to join in the prayers for Zöe. Then we waited. People from local churches contacted me to say that they were praying for her and would join in our prayer day. Many of them said they would pray for both Zöe and Miranda. Strangers from all religions sent me messages to say that they were sure she would be healed. We all waited.

Rudi's mother and youngest brother travelled from Bordeaux to see us. Naturally, Zöe's granny wanted to be with her and Miranda as much as possible. Rudi and his brother went to the Mormon Temple together to pray for Zöe.

When they came back, they took Zöe out and bought her a couple of little Russian hamsters. Zöe had always loved animals and wanted a pet. We bought an exercise ball for the hamsters and a marvellous cage with lots of tubes and a wheel. The hamsters were very sociable and loved to be picked up and stroked. The children loved them.

Our friend Pauline decided to buy a puppy, which she could share with Zöe. It would live at her house but she would bring it over regularly. It was a beautiful black and white border collie which she named Caz. Miranda was very nervous of the puppy but Zöe and her friends loved her a lot. She came to see us regularly and we bought her a name-tag and rubber bone.

We took Zöe to see a hospital specialist on January 27th. He told us that the tumour seemed to be spreading more. There was less feeling around Zöe's eyes. Our own doctor came quite regularly to see Zöe. Usually she was nice to him and sometimes told him a joke or rhyme but at other times she would not co-operate. She had seen too many doctors. He told us that people at his church would be joining in the prayers for Zöe too.

Our friend from the Social Services came to see us as well. She offered us games and books for children about dying but we would not take them. As she left, she told us that many of the people at the Social Services office were going to take part in Zöe's prayer day.

Sunday February 6th was the big prayer day. Zöe woke up and was sick. It was the fourth time she had been sick that week and we were worried. Her eyes looked very bloodshot and her face and throat seemed swollen. Rudi and Miranda stayed at home with her. I went to church to pray for Zöe and stood up to explain that although she was very ill with a brain tumour; two blessings had been given saying that she would recover. I said that people all over the world were praying and fasting for a miracle to happen. Many people stood up and spoke wishing Zöe well and everyone prayed. There was no more we could do now - her life was in God's hands.

When I went home after church, Zöe seemed a lot brighter. She was out of pain and was feeling cheerful. She did lots of drawing and spent most of the afternoon zooming around in the machine from The Mary Sheridan Centre. I really felt that the prayers had helped.

Zöe went to school for a while the next day. She seemed very bright still and not at all tired. We went to Whitstable beforehand and bought a collar for "Caz" the dog and a squeaky lamb-chop. Whilst Zöe was at school I took Miranda to the doctors for a pre-school booster and she was very well-behaved. It was good to have such a positive day. People from our church came to see us again and others phoned. Many of them now firmly believed Zöe would be healed. Rudi and I were very hopeful as well.

However, by Wednesday Zöe was being very sick. Her legs were wobbly and her speech slurred. The doctor came and said her bowel muscles were not working properly and this was probably the cause of the sickness – the body waste was coming up not going down. I felt so angry with God for not healing Zöe and for letting her get worse. The next day she could not even stand for one second. Her eyes were bloodshot and she was losing the feeling inside her mouth. When I gave her tablets she could not tell if she had swallowed them or not. Rudi collected some equipment for us to use to help Zöe when she tried to eat.

I also had more problems with Miranda. She still kept bending her legs in a C-shape so that her knees went backwards and clicked and I was scared she would break her legs. She had also started to be sick but I was not sure why. There was a meeting about which school Miranda should go to, and her playgroup leader, called in to tell me about it. The news was that Miranda could start at the local autism unit in a couple of weeks after all. I felt sad to see her leave The Mary Sheridan Centre but happy that she was going to the school of our choice.

Despite all the illness, we went to Butlins at Bognor Regis in the February half-term because Zöe wanted to go there. The children loved the amusement arcades and Miranda loved the Mr Blobby see-saw which she went on over and over again. Zöe slept a lot in the chalet and Rudi stayed with her whilst I took Miranda out. Zöe was still being very sick but there was not much we could do about it.

The main reason Zöe had wanted to come to Butlins was to see Timmy Mallet. He was a wonderful character from children's television and she loved watching him. We missed his first show because Zöe was asleep. When we went to the second show the queues were so long that we did not think we would be allowed in. I spoke to a redcoat and they arranged for Zöe to meet Timmy Mallett before the show. He signed her "Mallet's Mallet" for her – a large foam hammer-type object! Then she stayed to watch the show with Rudi. Miranda and I joined them for the last 15 minutes. The girls loved it when he sprayed the audience with a water gun and when he hit people with the Mallett. I was so pleased that Zöe was able to meet him and see his show. It meant a lot to her.

We all went to watch the dancing in the evening. Miranda kept approaching different children and trying to get them to dance with her. She could hardly speak so the children did not always understand what she wanted but she led them onto the dance floor by their hands and showed them how to dance. Five children danced with her and five ran away. Then she found a little boy whom she particularly liked. She would not let go of his hand and I had to separate them.

His father said. "She must be American - that's what the American women do – once they find a man they don't let him go!"

We came home on the Friday - it had been good to get away for a few days. We received a letter from a lady in Hampshire. She had read our appeal for prayers in the Daily Telegraph and she told us that children at her Baptist church were praying. They had all written little messages and prayers for Zöe and made her get-well cards. One little girl ended her prayer with "Are Men?" We were delighted to receive all the letters but somehow I felt that our miracle just was not going to happen. We left Miranda with a friend in the afternoon so that the house would be peaceful and Zöe could sleep. Zöe was very sick again, dribbling continuously and still not able to swallow properly.

Miranda started school on Tuesday 22nd February. It should have been a major event and I should have at least taken her photo, but all I could think about was Zöe. It had snowed outside and was very pretty so I took Miranda to school in a pushchair. If we were walking she would run away. Two friends offered us a lift to the school but it was a pleasure to walk. Miranda seemed very happy to be going to school but when I left her she cried and refused to take her coat off. She was very attached to her red coat and liked to keep it on if she was not at home. She also wanted to come home at 2 p.m. but school did not finish until 3 p.m. However, Miranda settled down eventually and had a fairly good day. After a while, going to school became part of Miranda's routine and she seemed to really enjoy going there.

At the end of February I went to Lyons, the funeral directors to ask about funerals. I also Zöe bought some white clothing. If she was going to die I wanted her to be buried in white as was the custom at our church. I had to be prepared for the worse. The doctor came that afternoon and told us that Zöe was in the final stages. A few of our friends decided to tell their children that Zöe was going to die. They wanted to prepare them so it would not be such a shock.

The following Monday, our doctor was meant to come but I phoned and cancelled him. We still wanted to make the most of every moment with Zöe. The weather was mild and spring-like so we took her to Howletts Zoo. She really enjoyed seeing all the animals especially the monkeys, apes and tigers. Afterwards, I took her to the seaside. We sat and watched the seagulls and looked at the view. A man was collecting pebbles from the beach for his greenhouse and he asked me about Zöe. I walked over to him and told him about her and he cried. Zöe never noticed because we were behind her. I wanted her to stay as happy and calm as possible - I did not want her to know that the end of her life was near. If she realised that death meant separation from us, it would be very, very difficult for her.

March came and day by day things seemed more difficult. Zöe asked to go to Whitstable shopping and bought presents for many of the people she loved. We carried on going to all the familiar places: the fields, the sea, shops and of course school. Visitors continued to come and see us but it was difficult for Zöe to communicate with them as her speech had gone. I took Zöe to a birthday party but she was unable to join in the games and just had to sit and watch everyone.

She went to school regularly for story time. Rudi would carry her into the classroom. All the children wanted to sit next to Zöe. They wanted to look after her and to help her sit up. One little boy at school especially loved her - he wanted to give her a special present but had nothing. He made his long black shoe-laces into a necklace for her and went home without any laces. Previously he had given her a wrapped-up door-wedge as a present.

Zöe was usually exhausted by late afternoon. Miranda would come home from school and immediately be in the way because she made such loud, happy noises most of the time. She was enjoying school and seemed happier. Zöe wanted to sleep and would be grumpy because Miranda kept her awake. Different people would come and take Miranda out. It was a dreadfully sad and frustrating situation.

We arranged a birthday party for Zöe on Saturday 19th March. We were scared that she would die before her seventh birthday on March 28th. She was finding it difficult to breathe and seemed to be wheezing slightly. I was very worried that she was losing her sight as well. Despite her physical deterioration she was quite chirpy and asked us if we would dye her hair red. She had always loved red hair possibly because of "The Little Mermaid." We decided to do it and Zöe was very pleased with the result.

We took Zöe to Tesco and bought two birthday cakes: a "Mr Blobby" one for Miranda and a "Clown" cake for Zöe. We decided to celebrate Miranda's birthday early as well as we felt that Zöe would die before April when Miranda would be five. We had asked a Clown to come to Zöe's party. She had seen him at another friend's party and thought he was wonderful. I tied lots of new brightly coloured windmills to the tree at the bottom of our garden.

We took Zöe to Argos and said she could choose some presents for her birthday. She bought herself a gold bracelet, a musical box, a gold dolphin on a chain, some felt-tip pens, a Mickey-mouse telephone and some pots of Play-Doh. She chose them carefully but did not play with any of them when we came home, in fact she never looked at them again except for the Mickey Mouse phone. Later I realised that she had bought them as gifts for us and not for herself. Rudi enjoyed drawing and would often use felt-tips to draw pictures for Miranda; I would wear the jewellery and Miranda would enjoy the phone and Playdoh.

The day of the birthday party arrived. I read Zöe a couple of stories and she tried to watch videos but I could tell that her sight was a lot worse. The clown arrived at 1.30 and he was fabulous! Miranda liked him and led him around the room by his hand. Then everyone else arrived and Miranda panicked so a friend took her away. It was sad that she missed the party but she could not cope with all the people. Zöe sat on her favourite green velvet armchair with everyone around her. The clown was excellent - the last time he had seen Zöe she was a healthy happy little girl and it must have been hard for him to see her so ill.

He did lots of magic tricks, balloon modelling and told jokes. He involved all the children, especially Zöe and did not do any games where they had to run around. Everyone laughed and enjoyed themselves but deep down we all knew this was Zöe's goodbye party. Miranda came back when the party was over. She had been taken to watch a hockey match and had loved it! Zöe was very tired and went to bed when everyone had gone.

We kept reading Zöe stories to amuse her. It seemed that the sight in her right eye as well as in her left one was deteriorating. I tried to talk to her about how she was feeling but she would not talk about being ill and just wanted to listen to stories, tapes and videos.

Pauline brought her the most wonderful present. It was a mobile made of crystals and we hung it in front of the window. They would catch the light and make rainbows appear around the room. Zöe could see the lights and the effect was magical.

Zöe enjoyed going out in the car for short rides and I was pleased that we lived in such a pretty area especially at this time of the year. Her sight was deteriorating and I wanted her to see as much beauty as possible before she lost it completely. On March 27th we took her over to Olive and Keith's house for a change of scenery. She sat in a chair facing their beautiful garden. It was good to go there but sad to see Miranda and Joel running around whilst Zöe could do nothing. She never complained.

Zöe was seven on March 28th. Relatives and friends called in to see her and she was very happy to see them and had a laugh. Afterwards she was tired and wanted to sleep. Miranda wanted to go out and went home with my sister.

A district nurse came a couple of days later with a syringe drive for Zöe. She was given an anti-sickness drug and morphine for any pain she might feel. It was terrible to see Zöe after this as she seemed to struggle for breath. She lapsed in and out of consciousness and pointed to "milk" on the chart with pictures that Rudi had made for her. She could not swallow so we just kept her mouth and lips moist with milk jelly.

On Tuesday March 31st the doctor came and told us that Zöe was going to die that day. Miranda had gone to school and I felt worried that she had not said goodbye to Zöe. She did not understand what was happening.

The doctor gave Zöe an injection to make her feel more comfortable and she slept. We were not sure if she could hear anyone. It was my sister Olive's birthday and she called in to read Zöe an Enid Blyton story. Close family and friends came to say goodbye to Zöe. After they had gone, Rudi and I could do little but sit with Zöe and tell her we loved her.

At one point I stood and looked out at the garden for a moment and saw a small green and yellow bird wedged inside the bird-feeding tube hanging from the Windmill Tree. I ran outside and unhooked the tube and tried to get the bird out. I thought it was dead but it made its way to the top of the tube and flew away, high up into the sky. I wondered if this was a symbol of Zöe's release from all her suffering.

At 1.30 on March 31st 1994 Zöe died.

Chapter 9 – Postcard from Heaven

April 1994 – May 1997

How can you explain what life is like when all hope has gone? Rudi and I were overwhelmed with grief and totally exhausted. Reminders of Zöe were everywhere we looked and it was very hard to cope with life now that she was not there. No words are shocking enough to describe the void left in our lives after Zöe died. It was strange to see other people's lives carrying on and time still moving forward. Everything felt very unreal. At first I felt as if I was surrounded by a giant bubble and floating around in the real world but not part of it. Everything I did seemed part of an act in a giant play and at times I wondered if God was the director. My heart and my feelings were removed from my actions

However, I felt that because Zöe had been bright and positive I should be too. If I cried I felt that I was letting her down by giving in to my grief. She had lost her life and I still had mine. I owed it to her to live my life in a positive way and make the most of it. I felt torn apart, pulled between positive thinking and utter despair.

Most of all I missed being able to touch Zöe. I missed cuddling her and looking after her. I felt that nothing I could ever do would matter as much as looking after Zöe. However, I knew that the worst thing I could do would be to give-up with life and do nothing.

A couple of days after Zöe's death we were at Olive and Keith's house. Miranda played with a family of little dolls: a father, mother and two little children one of which had red hair like Zöe's just before she died. Miranda would continually remove this doll from the rest and put it on a shelf. I kept putting it back with the other dolls. Then Miranda picked up the doll, opened the door and threw it outside. "Bye-Bye Zöe" she called out. We all felt upset but it was Miranda's way of telling us that she knew Zöe had gone.

After that Miranda came and sat on my lap for a very long time and gave me a cuddle as if to tell me that she was still here and needed me.

Zöe's funeral was beautiful and crowds of people attended. We thought of it as a celebration of Zöe's life and the church was adorned with hundreds of daffodils. Miranda stayed with a friend during the service as she would not have understood what was happening. A few days later we took Miranda to Zöe's grave. We called the grave "Zöe's garden" and Miranda understood that it was a special place.

Miranda started to pull her hair out and her eczema worsened. She was often stressed anyway and we wondered how Zöe's death would affect her. She asked us to draw pictures of birthday parties and would often say "Zöe". She liked us to draw Zöe with other children or with her favourite TV characters. We were pleased that she wanted to remember Zöe on happy occasions such as birthdays.

For a while after Zöe's death the children stopped playing outside our house and then gradually they appeared on their bikes. I found it very hard to see them and to know that Zöe would never be playing with them again. It was also difficult to go around the toy shops and Zöe's favourite places without her by my side.

I removed the windmills and the old bird feeder from the Windmill Tree at the bottom of our garden. A few days later, for the first time ever a beautiful branch of blossom appeared on the tree.

British Telecom had raised lots of money for Zöe and we distributed it among the charities and places that had helped her and Miranda. We had Zöe's name added to a golden tree of life at Ronald McDonald House. Next to her name was the name of the friend who had died just before her – he had often gone for his radiotherapy at the same time as Zöe, so that they could sit and talk.

The infant school planted a magnolia tree in remembrance of Zöe and the children in her class made us a book of memories. I enjoyed being at the school with the children but found it difficult because Zöe was not there. I helped with swimming lessons, sports and singing. One little boy asked me how Zöe had got to Heaven. Another one asked me if I had swapped Zöe for Miranda.

All the people who had cared for Zöe were deeply affected by her death and everyone grieved in their own way. Rudi was heartbroken and I felt his sadness as well as my own. I had a lot of nightmares about Zöe dying for months after her death. In some dreams I was able to cuddle Zöe and hold her again but then she would disappear and I would be searching for her. In other dreams she would be dying again and I would wake up sweating. In one particular dream I was with some new friends and Zöe walked into the room. I was very pleased to see her and told my friends that this was my daughter and she was alive again. I introduced her to them but then she disappeared.

Life seemed strange and religion seemed confusing. I occasionally still went to the Mormon church but believed less and less in the doctrines they taught there. I was very angry with God, if he existed, because Zöe had not been healed. I was not angry with the people who had given her false healing blessings – they had only said what they wanted to happen.

A beautiful blossom tree was planted outside the church in Zöe's memory. I remembered the time in London when a little girl visited Zöe and they played in the blossom as it fell from the trees.

I joined a local Church of England morning group which many of my friends attended. Their children had played with Zöe at school and they understood a little of what I was going through. I started to attend a "Morning Prayer" service at the little stone church across the field from where we lived, St.Alphege, Seasalter. It was peaceful and quiet. I was unsure what I believed but I felt if anything could restore my faith, going to this little church would. Only a few people attended and sometimes we would sit in silence for a few moments and listen to the birds singing outside and the trees rustling. It was therapeutic and calming. I asked if Zöe's name could be written in the remembrance book they kept at the church.

Christmas was very difficult, especially hearing the words of the Christmas carol "Away in the Manger." Tears rolled down my face when they sang, "Bless all the children in thy tender care. Lead them to heaven to live with you there." I left the carol concert.

On May 24th 1995 we had a ceremony in Whitstable in remembrance of Zöe. It was held at Duncan Down, a large open area of land near Whitstable windmill. My father had arranged for a bench to be placed there with Zöe's name engraved into the seat in memory of her. From Duncan Down there were lovely views of Whitstable, the sea and the windmill, all the places Zöe had loved. Besides my family, many of Zöe's school friends went to the ceremony and the local press took pictures. It was a wonderful occasion and would have meant a lot to Zöe. Miranda understood that the bench was "Zöe's seat" and she seemed pleased to remember her sister.

Time seemed to pass by quickly. At one time Miranda seemed to be looking for Zöe. She would point to children who vaguely resembled her sister and ask me "Zöe?" I would say "no, not Zöe" and Miranda would say "Zöe Jesus." I felt she did not understand what had happened to her sister. Miranda carried on thinking about Zöe and would often ask me to write down her name and to write down the names of all the other children they had played with together.

Towards the end of 1996 I decided to take Miranda to St.Alphege, Seasalter's family service which was held at her school. The Church of England music seemed very loud and modern compared to the music at the Mormon church and Miranda loved it. The atmosphere was also more relaxed and if Miranda made noises (which she did quite often) it was not a problem. We started going there regularly.

At home Miranda would dance to praise music in the kitchen and she became really excited when certain hymns came on such as "Shine Jesus Shine" and "Amazing Love." I remembered one doctor telling us that Miranda would never be religious because she was autistic. I wondered how that doctor defined "religious." Church music seemed to inspire Miranda in a way that no other music did.

Rudi eventually left the Mormon church and joined "the school church" as Miranda called it. He played his keyboard in the music group and enjoyed the variety of hymns there. It was good to all be together again on a Sunday. We enjoyed the community spirit and made many good friends.

On April 2nd 1997, I went to a church discussion group at someone's house. We talked about near-death experiences and dying. I became very negative and admitted that I had doubts about God existing at all. Rudi had asked Zöe to pass a secret word back to him (that only they knew) so he could be sure that she lived on in the after-life but he had heard nothing. Zöe had not appeared to me and I was not confident that she was alive in Heaven or anywhere else. I told everyone that I felt angry that God had not given me any feeling or sign that Zöe was fine and at peace. When I said this I had a feeling that something was going to happen. The people at the group said they would pray for me!

Two days later a child who lived nearby knocked on my door and asked if he could play with Miranda. We had known him for several years and he was nearly eight years old, the same age as Miranda. He ignored all of Miranda's toys and walked over to the CD player. Then putting on the headphones, he listened to a song called "I Believe" sung by Robson and Jerome. He wrote something on my telephone pad and told me he was going home.

After he left I read his note. It was written on one side of the paper only, just like a postcard would be written. The message said, "To Mum. I am in Heaven so I will see you. I can see you there. I want to see you again".

I was pleasantly shocked and immediately thought about the time when I had walked across a field with Zöe and she had asked me if she could send me a postcard from Heaven. I felt this was the postcard. It was a message from Zöe to me and an answer to prayers.

I phoned the little boy's mother and she had no idea why he would have written me a message. Later he came round to play again and I asked him why he had written the note. He said a feeling had come over him that he should write those words on one side of the paper for me.

I told a few people about the message. Some thought that it was an answer to prayers or a sign from Zöe. Others thought it was coincidence that the little boy had written the note to me just a couple of days after the prayers. There were many things that I would never know for sure and questions that might never be answered but I knew that it felt better to believe than to be filled with bitterness, doubts and fears. I had hope and I wanted to have my faith back as well and to believe that I had received a postcard from Heaven.

Chapter 10 – Just Miranda

April 1994 – December 1999

When she first started school, Miranda had been reluctant to put down the little objects she carried everywhere. This was a problem as her hands needed to be empty so she could do some work. She had kicked, screamed and held on to her little toys tightly at first but gradually let the teachers take them away during school hours. She usually carried a little doll with blonde hair, a rabbit and a cassette cover wherever she went. The cassette cover was the biggest problem as she was always dropping it in water or tearing it. The teachers kept her little toys and cassette cover near to her in the classroom at first so that she knew they were safe but gradually I was able to get her to leave them at home. Miranda could do so much more when her hands were empty.

She was generally very happy at school and enjoyed learning. The order and routines at school seemed to help Miranda feel secure in a confusing world and the teaching staff were excellent. There were sixteen children at the autism unit - all affected by autism in different ways. Their social interaction and speech skills varied a lot as did their behaviours and abilities. Some children were quite anxious and very withdrawn. Others were calmer and happier. Every child was very individual and they all needed a lot of help.

Miranda was progressing slowly. She enjoyed doing jigsaws especially ones of the alphabet. She loved looking at letters and had an alphabet frieze around her bedroom wall. She would bounce up and down on the bed reciting the alphabet. She could say quite a few words from the frieze such as "cat, dog, duck, apple, pig, elephant and jelly" and even learnt to spell them with large plastic letters. She was also singing nursery rhymes a lot: "Baa, Baa, Black Sheep, Humpty Dumpty" and many more. Her words were not very clear but I could understand her.

She gradually learned to spell and played matching words and pictures games on the computer. Her computer skills were very good for her age. Every day she seemed to be learning more and more nouns. She did not understand the "little in-between words" in a sentence such as "the," "and" or "even." Words that did not create a picture in her mind seemed to be too difficult to grasp. She mainly used single words and rarely said a whole sentence. She could not follow a conversation when people were talking but listened out for words she knew. Miranda also learned to write but she hated writing and her letters were large and untidy. For a long time she did not like drawing either but loved to watch other people draw – then suddenly she started to draw pictures by herself.

She became very interested in times-tables and in the mornings before school sometimes we would sit and write them out. Other times she would bounce up and down saying "12, 24, 36, 48 etc." She had been learning them by listening to cassettes of children singing times-tables. She did not always retain the information she learned maybe she did not understand the concepts behind what she was learning. She gradually seemed to lose her ability to count and within a few months seemed to have forgotten the times-tables she had loved to recite.

Miranda was usually quite happy at home but going out shopping with Miranda was a big problem. She liked to go to our local shop but if we took her elsewhere we would have problems. If I took her out in a pushchair she would push her feet down on the ground to stop the pushchair moving whenever she wanted to go somewhere different. If she was on reins she would pull me off balance. If I let Miranda walk freely she would go where she wanted to go which was not where I necessarily wanted to go. There were several occasions when she laid on the floor and screamed in shops because she could not have the toy or jigsaw that she wanted. As she got bigger I found it more difficult to pick her up. She would wiggle, go floppy, kick me or head-butt. On several occasions people, usually men, came over to offer me help me and I was very grateful. Sometimes I just needed someone to hold the pushchair steady whilst I strapped her back in. Other times it took two of us to pick her up and carry her somewhere safe so she could not bang her head on the pavement in temper. Sometimes people would help to pick up all the toys and shopping for me that Miranda had scattered all over the pavement. It was much easier to go out when Rudi was off work or at weekends and there were two of us to handle her than it was to manage her alone.

Miranda had become very possessive of Rudi. She hated it when he talked to anyone other than herself and if he was on the phone she would put her hand over his mouth or gently kick him to tell him she was jealous. She did not like him talking to me or to any visitors who came either and this was a big problem. If we sat down with people she would be so disruptive that we could not enjoy a relaxed conversation. She particularly liked to make loud noises each time the visitors spoke so that we could not hear them. Sometimes Rudi and I would sneak away and talk in the kitchen or bedrooms so that Miranda did not keep interrupting us. We often talked to friends in the garden or sat outside in their cars and talked. Punishing Miranda had little effect - she was so determined.

At home, I did lots of drawing for Miranda and made little clothes out of blue-tac for her Polly Pocket dolls. She enjoyed videos, music and the computer. She loved dolls of all types: Barbie dolls, Cabbage Patch ones and of course "Little Quints." She especially liked to choose dolls to play with which looked like herself or Zöe.

Miranda would be very upset if she heard a child cry or talk in a high-pitched voice. She took a dislike to one particular child at her school who was very nice and quiet. Miranda was scared to be in the same room as her but no-one knew why. When Miranda was put into another class she developed a fear of a child in her new class. Again the child was a nice, quiet, inoffensive child. When Miranda moved class again she chose another child to be scared of and avoid. It seemed that Miranda always picked one child whom she could be scared of and dislike.

Miranda had developed a love of "Barney the big Purple dinosaur," a television character and she would often sing his song "I love you, you love me" etc. Miranda knew the word "love" was good and everywhere she went would point to hearts and say "love." She picked up lots of the products at our local supermarket and searched for heart symbols on the packaging. She enjoyed painting rainbows and hearts and liked me to draw them for her. This seemed a very good phase to go through. She gave me wonderful cuddles and was a very loving, happy child at home when there was just Rudi and me around.

We worried a lot about Miranda's eczema. Antibiotics cleared it but as soon as the course finished the eczema would come back again. Creams helped but did not heal it. It meant that she was itchy and uncomfortable at school and we felt sorry for her. She often came home with blood on her clothes where she had made the eczema bleed. Her little hands were very sore and scratched.

In the mornings before school, Miranda and I had developed a routine. First of all we would watch a video, then she would have a bath whilst I sang her nursery rhymes. After that we would get dressed, then type words on the computer and do some drawing. The morning routine helped her to relax before school. Without the same routine every day she would become very stressed and anxious. I realized how much more secure Miranda felt when she knew what was going to happen each day.

Towards the end of 1995 Miranda was very ill. She would be sick for a few days and then be fine again. Then the sickness came back. She could not tell us if she had a headache as her speech was not good enough to explain to us how she felt. We were very, very worried as we remembered all the times when Zöe was sick as a child. Eventually our doctor referred her to Canterbury hospital and we went there in April 1996 just after Miranda's seventh birthday. As usual we had a long wait and Miranda moaned. The hospital doctor said that Miranda had no signs of a brain tumour and he saw no reason for her sickness. He said children often had unexplained sickness and that the sickness would probably disappear all on its own. I felt annoyed with the doctor and the whole visit seemed a waste of time but strangely enough a little while later the sickness did disappear on its own and Miranda seemed to be healthy again!

In 1996 the Social Services introduced us to a family who could look after Miranda at their house on alternate Saturday afternoons. The parents were very easy-going and the three children were all eager to befriend Miranda and play with her, so we were very pleased with the arrangement. Miranda loved going to see the new family and spent many happy afternoons playing at their house, dressing up the dog in tea-towels and putting hats on everyone!

At home, Miranda had very few friends as most of the children she knew had outgrown her or had gradually stopped coming to visit. They played games that she could not join in or understand - they were growing-up. Miranda, to some extent, stayed like a young child. Sometimes I felt Miranda was lonely but at other times she seemed to prefer her own company. She often watched the neighbours through the window and would tell me, using just one or two words, what they were doing or where they were going. I was pleased she went to the local church and school as she saw lots of children in both those places although she did not play with them. I felt sad that Miranda had no sister to look after her or to play games with.

Miranda was still wearing nappies at seven years old and no-one could persuade her to use a toilet. I was embarrassed about having such a big child in nappies. One bright summer's day we decided to bribe her with a visit to Toys 'R' Us. We had tried bribery many times before but it had never worked. This time it did, maybe because she was in an especially good mood.

We told her "No nappy. Yes knickers, yes toilet, yes Miranda go to Toys 'R' Us."

After a few moans, she took off her nappy, put on a pair of knickers and went to the toilet. We were very pleased and surprised. We took her to Toys 'R' Us as promised. Miranda never asked for a nappy again and from that day onwards she was toilet-trained. We were extremely pleased and no doubt all the teachers at her school were too. It was great to have a seven year old who did not wear nappies. Best of all we did not have to take her to Toys 'R'Us every time she went to toilet!

We took Miranda out most weekends and during the school holidays despite her problems with noise and her fear of small children. We visited all the local shopping centres, parks, gardens, zoos and seaside places. Miranda loved amusement arcades especially sitting in miniature cars. We always ended up in McDonalds on our days out. We went on various holidays in England and even took Miranda back to Disneyland Paris a couple of times. Although, this all sounded wonderful, it was not. The reality was that Miranda became more and more stressed when we were outside.

She was tense all the time and often had her hands over her ears just in case she passed any noisy children. If they cried or screamed then she would cry and scream too, often in exactly the same pitch of voice as they used. If they did not stop crying she would become very upset and have a tantrum hurting herself and occasionally hurting us, with frustration. We tried to explain that babies cried because they were hungry or that children sometimes cried because they wanted something but could not have it. No explanation would help.

She made continuous loud noises whilst we were out to block out other sounds and many trips ended in tantrums and tears because she saw a baby crying in a pushchair. She was also very upset if our routine changed or if a shop we usually visited closed. She set-up routines wherever we went and if we returned to a shopping centre she liked to visit all the shops in exactly the same order as on the previous visit. Our closest friends had a baby and Miranda was terrified of him in case he cried. She would not go to their house and would not come downstairs if they came to our house.

In 1999 we started looking at secondary schools for Miranda as she had to change schools at age eleven. Rudi and I wanted to find another school with caring staff who would motivate Miranda and help her to progress in the same way as she had at Joy Lane School's Autism Unit. We were not worried about academic achievements but more that Miranda would be happy and secure. We were given a list of schools for children with special needs and started to look around them all. There seemed to be no local secondary schools with autism units. The schools on the list fell into two categories: ones for children with severe learning difficulties and ones for children with moderate learning difficulties. It was not clear to us what the differences were between the two types of schools until we started to visit them.

We went to a very good moderate learning difficulty school. Most of the children there seemed to understand what the teachers were saying to them and could follow a fairly normal lesson with some help. Some of the children seemed to have emotional problems or behavioural problems. Others could not keep up at a mainstream school through no fault of their own. Some had learning disabilities and a few had physical disabilities. They were a mixed bunch of children. The school was very good and the teachers had very positive ideas. We realized that unfortunately Miranda would be out of her depth at this school because her understanding of language was so bad. She would not understand what the teacher was saying or follow any of the lessons. Nor would she be able to socialize or talk with other children and teachers.

We were told that Miranda was much more suitable for a severe learning difficulty school. Her understanding of language and speech was about the same as that of a two year old, although her spelling of simple everyday words was much better. She was working towards level one in most of her school subjects. We looked at more schools and were impressed by how caring and positive the staff were at most of them. The schools we looked at for children with severe learning difficulties tended to take children with mixed disabilities, including autism. It upset Rudi and me to see so many children having to cope with physical disabilities at these schools as well as having learning difficulties. We wondered what Zöe would have been like if she had lived? We sat outside a couple of the schools and fought back tears for all the children who were physically or mentally disabled but especially for our own. Why was life so cruel?

Eventually we chose a school for Miranda where all the children and teachers seemed happy and relaxed. I first looked around it with my sister Olive, as Rudi was away working. We both loved the atmosphere straightaway and agreed that any child could be happy there. There were bright pictures on the walls and the school buildings were very light and modern. I disliked any school buildings that were dark - they reminded me of the old-fashioned institutions which existed in my childhood where disabled children were hidden away from society.

Just before the Millennium celebrations we decided to move house. Rudi had started to work at home and no longer commuted to London so one of our bedrooms had become an office for him as well as a spare room. Relatives visited us from France and Australia that year and suddenly we felt short of space. We just had one downstairs room and really needed another one. Miranda hated it when everyone sat and talked. She liked to be able to watch the television with peace and quiet all around her. She also liked to spread her books and videos across the floor in a certain order. If I tidied them she would put them all back again just as they were before. We needed more space and so did Miranda.

New houses were going to be built on the fields all around our house. The places where I had walked with the children would never be the same again. We had lost a long battle with the local council to keep our green fields. Everything was changing.

We decided to move before Miranda changed schools so she did not have a lot of upheaval all at once. We did not want to go far because we loved our area and had so many memories in Whitstable. We did not want to leave our family, friends, the church or the community that had been so kind to us and given us so much love and support.

At the top of the hill and across the field behind our house there had once been a caravan park where Zöe and Miranda had played. Now the play-park and caravans had gone and large new houses were being built on the site. We went to look at them and decided to move there. I liked the idea of moving to a place with good memories and it was not very far away. There would be a lot more space for Rudi and Miranda.

I looked out of the bedroom window as the New Millennium arrived and watched the fireworks over the sea. I wondered what the future would bring for us all and I felt excited but worried about all the changes ahead.

Chapter 11 - A New Millennium

April 2000 – March 2003

At the school where Zöe used to go the children and staff created a beautiful Millennium garden. A seat inside was dedicated to her and a plaque inscribed with the words "Zöe – a child of the spring." The garden was designed to encourage wildlife, with a pond, many plants and a sundial. Children could go and feed the birds in this little garden. Zöe would have loved it.

In April 2000 we moved to our new house. Everyone wondered how Miranda would cope with the move because she hated change so much. However, as soon as she saw the television, her videos and all her toys she was fine. The extra rooms downstairs meant that she could sit in a separate room to us when visitors came. She could close the door and block out the noise of people talking.

Miranda started her new school several miles away and she is very happy there. She also attends a Technology College for part of the week. Several children from Miranda's school have their own classroom at the college and they join the mainstream school children for some of their lessons. Miranda has joined in computer lessons, music, dancing and assembly. Her understanding and abilities are similar to those of a very young child but she loves to learn and enjoys going to school.

It is March 2003 now, and Miranda is nearly fourteen years old. It's very early in the morning. I come downstairs and prepare the room for Miranda's morning routine. She is asleep in bed. She likes the room to be laid out in a certain way in the mornings. I move her little white table from one side of the room to the other. I put two biscuits in a pink dish for her. She will not eat them or anything else for breakfast but she likes them to be there. I pour out her orange squash into a Teletubbies glass and put the glass and dish onto a white tray, which I put onto the small white table.

I turn the television to Channel 4 and wind back the video tapes which she watched the night before. Each video tape has to be placed in a certain order on a pile at the other end of the room. The room always has to be this way or Miranda would be upset when she comes downstairs. She would also be upset if I gave her a different glass or dish.

Miranda always wears pink leggings and a pink or red sweatshirt with a picture of Minnie Mouse on the front. She hates to wear any other clothes and I have to constantly search for new pink and red clothes in her size with Minnie Mouse on the front. If I cannot find any I buy plain pink and red clothes and sew Minnie Mouse motifs onto them. She's worn Minnie Mouse clothes for years and will not wear different ones. At the college where she goes they have a black uniform. We tried to make her wear it but she refused. She became very upset and kept hitting herself - then she took the black clothes off anyway. We tried sewing Minnie Mouse motifs on the black clothes but she still would not wear them. She loves her pink clothes and has special permission to wear them when she goes to the college.

After Miranda gets dressed she goes to the bathroom. She always takes a green book with her. Miranda no longer has a bath as she is scared of the noise of the water draining down the plug-hole. I usually give her a quick wash with a flannel on school mornings. She uses the toilet and runs downstairs. I am not allowed to flush the toilet until she is at the bottom of the stairs as the noise of the toilet flushing frightens her. Downstairs, she sits and watches Channel Four. If there is any clapping or laughing she turns the volume down on the television. If a picture comes on the screen that frightens her, she turns on the teletext instead with just the Channel Four sound. We sit and look at the teletext for five minutes. When it's time for the adverts she immediately turns the television off.

Then she says "Dumbo" and I read her the story of Dumbo. She has had the same story every morning for about six years. I have almost memorized the words. She is happy and cuddles me whilst I read her the story. If I say a word wrong Miranda corrects me at once. She can read most of the words and she also knows the story off by heart though I am not sure if she fully understands it. She's added some of her own words to the story. At the end of one sentence about Dumbo going to the elephant tent she's written "To I will, oh perhaps practice laughing see what happened ha ha while tell like hmm whole too something else." I'm not sure what this means but Miranda knows. She's also made the story more positive. When it reads "Dumbo was sad" she's changed "sad" to "happy." When it says he was "no good" she's crossed out the "no" and made him good. After the story, I put the book back in exactly the same place as before. She keeps it under the television cabinet and does not like it to be moved.

When the story is finished Miranda says "move table." I move her little white table back to the other side of the room near the chair where she sits after school.

She runs into the hallway and gives me her trainers and socks. She can put them on herself but she likes me to do it for her. If she puts her socks on herself, half the time she will put the heel-part over her in-step. She gives me a big hug when I lean down to help her and laughs. She laughs a lot and makes happy noises. Then she puts her coat on and we go to the kitchen.

Miranda does not eat any breakfast and generally her diet is very limited. We know what Miranda should eat but she will not eat a balanced diet. Ever since she was a toddler she has refused to eat more than a few foods. Now the only foods she eats regularly are plain crisps, chips and cheese quavers. At her last school she used to eat cream crackers for lunch but she suddenly stopped eating them. Very occasionally she will eat green jelly or tea-finger biscuits. Miranda used to love McDonalds but is scared to go there now in case there are babies crying or small children making a noise.

Recently, when we tried again to make Miranda eat ordinary meals she stopped eating altogether and nearly fainted. Miranda's face, ankles and stomach seemed to be swelling slightly. We took her to the doctor, then to the hospital for blood tests. Miranda was puzzled by the blood tests and said to me afterwards, "Miranda no red arm Miranda beige arm."

Unfortunately the blood tests showed that Miranda had anaemia and a protein deficiency. We saw a dietician and we also looked on the internet for ideas of how we could supplement her diet. Now every day I give Miranda vitamins, iron medicine and health drinks containing protein. She will take these because she categorizes them as "medicines" in her mind and not as "food".

At 7.30 a.m. every morning we go into the kitchen. Miranda says "orange medicine" and gives me a white spoon. She expects to have all her medicines and drinks at certain times of the day and will remind me if I am late giving her one. Her iron and protein levels are improving and she is much better than she was a few months ago.

I do the washing-up. Miranda likes me to wash the various cups and dishes in a certain order and then dry them up in a certain order. She likes to help put things away and then she rinses out the sink and washing-up bowl. She cannot stand to have any bubbles left in the bowl or sink. She loves to be helpful.

She hears Rudi upstairs in his office and calls out to him "Good morning Rudi, Good morning Sally, Good morning Miranda". She always wishes us all a good morning including herself.

Miranda and I go back into the living room. We sit down on the settee and do drawing and writing until her school minibus or taxi comes. This is Miranda's most talkative time of the day. When Miranda was little I discovered that she would be much less anxious if I did drawings for her whilst she was waiting to go out. Gradually as Miranda's vocabulary increased she would tell me what to draw and then what to write. Over the years this has become a way for her to share with me all the things that she is thinking about.

Today she wants to talk about her holiday in Blackpool in August 1999. She loves dates and will tell me the exact date and day of the week that we went anywhere. She tells me the door number on the chalet, the names of the shops we visited, the toys she collected at McDonalds and many more facts about the holiday that I had forgotten. She speaks mostly in single words and really quickly. If she gets excited she shouts out the words. I have to jot down all the things she says. Then she is really happy. Miranda also wants me to draw the amusement arcades for her and tells me what to put inside them. Her vocabulary is better than my drawing. She wants me to draw cars, bikes, ski and skateboard machines, a rollercoaster and various other things.

Then she asks me to draw children and tells me exactly how they should look: "yellow hair, three eyelashes, one purple hair tie, purple jumper, butterfly on jumper, white collar, blue jeans, trainers with two straps and a happy toe" etc. She is very precise. The children I draw have happy or sad toes on their trainers. This refers to the shape of the front of their trainers. She has lots of little expressions like this and I understand most of them.

After this she talks about her favourite television characters "the Wombles" and I draw her seven favourite Wombles. She is obsessed with the Wombles and tells me all the videos they were in, the titles of each story, who produced the videos and the dates the various episodes were on television. She tells me to write "Castlevision blue gate" and I have to draw a blue gate. This is because there is a picture of a blue gate on some of the video covers. Miranda helps me to colour in the Wombles faces and tells me whether their ears should point up or down.

If I draw something wrong she says in a really sweet voice "silly mummy, never mind, try again." I talk to her as we draw. There are certain words she hates to hear. If I say "looks like" or "okay" she gets really angry. I'm not sure why she objects to me using these words. If she hears the word "breakfast" she will say "if the need." If she hears the word "together," she will say "living room." If she is very angry she will say "Bungo's birthday party" and if she is very happy she will say "Parsley's birthday party." Another child with autism we knew said, "foot hurts" whenever she was upset. I understand a lot of Miranda's coded speech.

About once a week Miranda talks about Zöe and tells me the names of all the children they played when they were little and what number houses they lived in. She calls her favourite dolls "Zae and Marinda" like "Zöe and Miranda."

Shortly after starting at her new school, Miranda seemed to become obsessed with Zöe. She talked about her every day and started looking at old photos of when they were small children. Then Miranda started to hide photos under the bed and in cupboards and look at them secretly. We found some photos torn in little pieces and others photos with clothes or legs coloured-in. First of all we were very angry. Then we realized that Miranda had destroyed or edited our photos because of the obsession she has about fashion and what people wear. She did not like the clothes that Zöe and her were wearing in some of our earlier photos so she changed or destroyed them. She hates to see bare arms or legs in the winter and will draw long sleeves or tights on the children in pictures. She also hates to see any pictures of herself as a toddler wearing a dress. We decided to lock our favourite photos away to and give Miranda her own set of childhood photographs. We wanted Miranda to be able to look at the photos whenever she wanted but obviously not to destroy our collection. Miranda still seems unsure of what has happened to her sister and often mentions her even though it's nine years since her death.

Last year she kept asking if children we had known in the past had died. She would say a name and then ask, "died?"
I would reply, "no, not died, moved to a different house."
She seemed to accept this and would say "only Zöe died." I found this very sad but Miranda was quite matter of fact about it.

Emotions confuse her. She does not always understand why people are sad or happy and if they are ill or sick she sometimes laughs then says "that's not funny." Children with autism have trouble working out how people are feeling.

At church Miranda saw an extract from the "Miraclemaker" where Jesus brings back a little girl to life. Later she asked "Where's Zöe?" Lots of people told her that Zöe was in Heaven which has puzzled her. She asked "Where's Heaven?" I probably confused her more by saying "Heaven like Care Bear Land. Jesus good and kind like Care Bears." This explanation helped for a while and then a few weeks later Miranda asked me "Care Bears dead? Clangers dead?" and told me to put her Care Bears and Clangers videos in the garage, out of sight.

We have taken Miranda to Zöe's grave several times and she calls it Zöe's garden. We do not think that she understands Zöe is buried there. I worry about how she views the subject of death. After a television documentary with mummies wrapped in cloths, which she happened to see, Miranda wrapped two dolls in kitchen roll and put them in the bin.

Every now and again, Miranda tells me that Zöe lives in a house with a green door, which has number 80 on the front. She tells me what Zöe is doing and makes up a life for Zöe that parallels her own. Recently she told us that Zöe goes to church in Maidstone. She also told us what shops Zöe goes to and that Zöe eats crisps but different crisps from Miranda.

Crisps are another of Miranda's obsessions at present. She only eats Walkers ready salted ones and cheese quavers but she collects one bag of every other type of crisps we can find. She checks the crisps drawer regularly to make sure we have not eaten any of her collection whilst she is at school. Crisps are quite cheap to collect, (much cheaper than coins or stamps). Whenever we go shopping the shop assistants look at all the crisps and ask "having a party?"

After, all our drawing and writing in the morning, Miranda goes off to school quite happily. The driver puts on various tapes or CDs for the students in the minibus to listen to. Miranda likes to hold the CD covers whilst the music is playing. If she does not like the picture on the cover she will tear out the offending bit. Usually it's because the coat the pop singer is wearing is the wrong colour or he has a hat on that she does not like. We all keep our precious CD covers away from Miranda as much as possible. Her own covers are full of holes where she has torn them.

Miranda knows the names of all the children she travels to school with and the names of most of the children at her school. She tells me what classes they go to and quite often what lessons she thinks they have. I am pleased she is interested in everything that goes on around her. During the last school holidays she said to me "school bus, box, wheelchairs." She wanted me to make a school bus for her dolls out of a shoe-box and especially to make a wheelchair entrance at the back so all the dolls could go for rides just like at school. Miranda also wanted me to make wheelchairs for some of her dolls. We made these out of cornflake boxes, using straws for the framework and silver foil paper for the wheels.

Miranda has always enjoyed school. We have a school/home book for her and I write in it what she has been doing at home and send it to school every morning. The teachers write what she has been doing at school and send the book back to me. This system is ideal as Miranda cannot speak enough to tell us in any detail what she has been doing or how she is feeling.

Miranda's speech and communication are still a major problem. She sees a speech therapist at school. Sometimes I dream that Miranda is standing with other children, laughing and having a normal, everyday conversation but this is only in a dream. In reality, when I take her out, she often stands next to people she likes but does not know what to say to them or what to do if they speak to her.

She has many different lessons – swimming, history, geography, French, mathematics, English, art, religious education etc. All lessons are designed so that she can understand them and cope with them. In mathematics, Miranda can add and subtract one and sometimes two digit numbers. Her skills vary from time to time as she regularly forgets a lot of what she learns. She understands different shapes but finds concepts like solid and flat very difficult to grasp. In French, she learned to say and to spell quite a few words - mostly colours and numbers. She likes to sit and cross out French words in her children's dictionary and write English words instead. She says "French wrong, English right.

Miranda especially enjoys the days when she can attend the Technology College in Margate. She is usually very relaxed and happy when she arrives. The taxi driver takes her from the car into the classroom. She would be unable to cross the road on her own safely and may not find her way to the classroom if she was alone. She goes into a base class with a few more children with learning difficulties.

A Learning Support Assistant takes her into the mainstream school for assembly, for music lessons and dancing. Miranda is easier to teach and calmer in the mornings for some reason. She's more lively and noisy in the afternoons. The staff know her so well that they can generally judge when it is best to integrate her with the mainstream pupils and when she is better to work alone.

Miranda used to go happily to a mainstream computer class but then she became rather bad-tempered and vocal when the work became too difficult and she kept turning the computers off. After a few months break and some extra work to make computing less frustrating for her she was taken back to the computer class again and reintroduced to the lessons. She is now quite successful at doing some computer tasks. She loves to search on Google for children's television characters and programmes.

She used to go to dancing lessons in a mainstream class too, but over a period of time she became unsettled and sometimes noisy at the wrong moments. It was decided that she should go to the lunchtime dancing club instead which she enjoys. The lunchtime dancing sessions are not so formal and Miranda has more freedom to express herself. She insists on taking along jeans and a t-shirt to change into. None of the other children change clothes for dancing club so this puzzles everyone. Normally, Miranda insists on wearing pink and red Minnie Mouse clothes but for dancing she has made different rules for herself. We wonder if she feels that she is performing like a celebrity and therefore needs a special outfit.

Miranda enjoys music lessons with the mainstream pupils. She has a lot of help and encouragement from other pupils, the teacher and her helper at school. She performed a version of a Wombles song to the class and everyone clapped. She is very fond of her music lessons and when she was very sick during a class she did not want to leave the lesson but wanted to carry on with the activity regardless of all the sick around her.

She has always loved hearing Rudi play on the keyboard at home and has her own little Early Learning Centre keyboard. Miranda is especially excited when Rudi's friends come to play music at our house. She thinks it's wonderful when they rehearse with keyboards, guitars and drums.

At school and at home Miranda likes to keep a diary which she types on the computer. She does not like to write by hand. Miranda likes to make lists of Wombles names in her diary every day and this has become rather repetitive. She is far more interested in writing about Wombles than writing about her daily life. Miranda's spelling is good. She will often spell out words to people if they cannot understand what she is saying.

Miranda enjoys reading but her understanding is limited. She can follow very simple factual stories designed for younger children with pictures but abstract stories are far more difficult for her. Her favourite books are catalogues of clothes and cartoon books. Unfortunately she tries to tear out any pictures that she does not like in books but she has been taught to fold the pages over and not to rip them out

Miranda does a form of Yoga at college which she finds quite a calming activity. At her last school the day often finished with relaxation to music. It is lovely to see children who are usually anxious or very active relaxing. Sometimes before Miranda goes home from college, she is asked to choose a CD. Her teacher lights a candle and Miranda sits and listens to the music whilst watching the flickering candle. She always chooses the same song – the hymn "Be Still in the Presence of the Lord."

The most difficult times at school have been when there were special activities such as Christmas parties, pantomines or shows. Miranda cannot always cope with the changes to the normal routine and the large amounts of children present. When this happens she sometimes has to stay behind in her classroom or I keep her at home for the day.

Miranda comes home at about 4 p.m. most days. When she arrives home she takes off her coat and shoes and goes into the living room. She switches on the television and waits for me to bring her oven chips, which are always in a turquoise green dish. I put these next to her cheese quavers, which are always in a yellow dish. She drinks 7up light, in a Thomas the Tank Engine glass.

We have two televisions in our living room. One is for Miranda and the other is for us. Miranda puts a DVD called "The Herbs" on our television about Parsley the Lion's birthday. She puts a "Mr Blobby" video on her television and puts a "Jellikins" comic on her lap and two "Hoobs" comics by her side. She has various books, comics and clothes catalogues arranged on the floor and chairs. Everything has to be in the same place every day. Then as soon as Miranda's "Mr Blobby" tape starts she begins to eat her chips. If I speak to her and ask her about school she will tell me what she did very briefly, for example she will say "school, dancing, library, goodbye." When she says goodbye she wants me to go out of the room so she can relax on her own for a few minutes. I go back in to see her every few minutes and pour her out another drink. She cannot open a bottle and pour one out herself. She is unable to unscrew the bottle tops and also is unable to judge how much to pour out.

If there are children playing outside Miranda will put headphones on to block out the noise of them playing. She hates to hear children's voices. It is amazing that she copes with the noise of children at school. If the telephone rings in the hallway and Rudi or I go to answer it, Miranda will shut the door to her room as she does not like to hear us talking.

Miranda asks me to sit down and draw pictures with her again. She will pester me until I draw what she wants. We are gradually redesigning the clothes in all our clothing catalogues and comics. Miranda puts white stickers over the outfits she dislikes and I redesign them. She tells me exactly what to draw - for example she will make flared trousers into straight ones; straight ones into flared ones and blue jeans into stripey trousers. She will ask me to draw pictures on plain t-shirts; change vests into coats and take off any hats. If Miranda could do the drawings all by herself she would possibly be a great designer as she has a marvellous eye for colour and detail. Miranda can take in much more visually than I can. She remembers what people were wearing at school, parties or in photos from years before.

Miranda has an even more remarkable trait regarding her memory of days and dates. We noticed that she would watch the video clips on "You've been Framed" and other television programmes and read out the dates on them. Then she would tell us if that day was a Friday or a Wednesday for example. Gradually we started to test her and realized that if we asked her what day of the week any date was during the 1990's she would tell us the correct day. She seems to have a calendar in her mind which covers all days from 1989 when she was born. She does not realize it is clever to tell us that a certain day in 1992 was a Thursday, for example. I'm not sure how the skill of memorizing days and dates could be used or even if Miranda will retain it but it's impressive.

Miranda has always looked forward to all the special days in the year. We celebrate most things in our house – birthdays, new year, valentine's day, red nose day, Easter, Halloween, fireworks day, Christmas and many other occasions. She is happy for people to come and see us when it is her birthday or if it is fireworks day. Miranda gets very excited about her birthday now. We usually have a party and about twelve children come. Most of them are teenagers. Quite a few adults come to Miranda's birthday parties as well. We think it's because we play some very good party games! "Pass the Parcel" is one of Miranda's favourites. Miranda loves it when everyone sings "Happy Birthday to Miranda and she thinks it's wonderful to blow out the candles on a cake. She usually rushes around the house laughing. She almost bounces off the walls with excitement and we have to calm her down. If she does not like a birthday present she will throw it away instantly or say "Don't like it." After a while, Miranda usually decides that her birthday party is over and then she will encourage everyone to leave. She is likely to tell various people "goodbye" and bring them their coats. She gets annoyed if anyone stays too long.

On a normal day, during the evening besides doing lots of drawing and writing with me, Miranda likes to listen to music and watch Children's videos. Sooty is one of her favourite videos. She also likes a wide range of music. Like most teenagers Miranda's moods vary but generally she is very happy. She makes a lot of noise, talks to herself and giggles a lot. She is often excited and will rush around the room laughing and jumping over the chairs.

When Rudi finishes work he sometimes sits and watches television. Miranda will then sit on the arm of his chair and rest her feet on his knees and laugh. She likes to sit with her dad and she shouts out the answers to a couple of simple questions he asks her about school and giggles a lot. If he asks her more than a couple of questions she will shout at him "no questions" and she will get cross. She also gets annoyed if she does not understand what he asking.

Holidays away from home are very difficult because of Miranda's fear of children and their voices. When we travel anywhere in our car we always have the same music playing for Miranda. It is a cassette called "Going to the Zoo." We have endured it for eight years now on all of our journeys! She panics if it does not work and on one occasion when we refused to put the cassette on, she shook and was sick.

Miranda spends a lot of the time on holiday watching videos and trying to do the same things as at home. We usually go to holiday camps or stay in a caravan. She loves dancing in the evenings and loud music at the holiday clubhouses. The music and cabarets will sometimes drown-out the other sounds that frighten her. If too many children are running around Miranda will become anxious and rush back to the caravan but otherwise she will relax and sometimes dance. She often finds a child she likes the look of on holiday and will follow her around. Frequently this is a child of about six years old who reminds her of Zöe at that age. I have to explain to the child and her parents that Miranda is harmless and just wants to stand near to them. This year we are going to take Miranda on holiday when most other children are still at school. We are hoping she will be willing to go out more in the daytime if everywhere is quieter and that she will feel less anxious if there are not so many children around.

Before Christmas, Miranda's fear of noise became so bad that she refused to go out shopping. This was after a few trips to Canterbury when we passed babies crying and children shouting. Miranda could not cope with this at all. First of all she would just stamp her feet and angrily jump up and down. Then she had terrible tantrums – crying, screaming, hitting herself, head-banging and throwing herself on the pavement. We decided to let Miranda have her way and stay indoors on Saturdays for a while. It is over four months now since she has been willing to go to Canterbury or any other big shopping centre.

It is hard to find a place that is quiet enough to take her and impossible to escape noise or other children. We have tried taking her out wearing industrial-type headphones to block out the noises around her but she is scared whenever she sees a small child in case it makes a noise. Miranda often puts her hands over her ears and makes a continual loud noise to try and block out other noises. If she hears the wind blowing, or sees a dog that might bark she will sometimes freeze on the spot or hide behind me. When we come home from anywhere she will continually say "no bell, no bell" as she is terrified that I will ring the front door bell.

Miranda is happy to be at home on Saturdays when she is not visiting her grandparents. On Sundays we go to church as usual but Miranda sits in a room away from the main service and we draw pictures. She can no longer cope with the noise and all the people in the main hall.

At home, we have occasional visitors and Miranda is happy about that as long as they do not stay too long. She will say "hello" to everyone when they arrive and then she will go in a different room, shut the door and ignore them. She does not like it when any visitors go into the same room as her especially if they talk.

Today, we go through the normal evening routine - Miranda plays her videos then goes to bed. She always says a goodnight prayer with me. We say the same words every night and pray for our family, our friends and of course, Zöe. It is nine years now since Zöe died but Miranda often mentions something about her as she is going to sleep. She is still very much alive in our hearts and will never be forgotten.

The Windmill Tree

Like the whispers of a summer breeze
The humming of the bumble bees
The rippling of the mountain streams
I hear your voice in all my dreams

But you are gone and life goes on
I stand alone – the strongest tree
As birds fly high and seagulls cry
Only willows weep for me

Be not afraid for I am here
My spirit lingers ever near
You cannot understand or see
But one day you will follow me

Sally Cazeaux